MICHELLE FAGONE

AIR FRYER ESSENTIALS

LOW CARB

adams media

AIR FRYER ESSENTIALS: LOW CARB
First published in Australia in 2022 by
Simon & Schuster (Australia) Pty Limited
Suite 19A, Level 1, Building C, 450 Miller Street, Cammeray, NSW 2062
First published in the United States in 2020 as *The "I Love My Air Fryer" Low-Carb Recipe Book* by
Adams Media, an imprint of Simon & Schuster, Inc.

10 9 8 7 6 5 4 3 2 1

Sydney New York London Toronto New Delhi
Visit our website at www.simonandschuster.com.au

Always follow safety and commonsense cooking protocols while using kitchen utensils, operating ovens and stoves, and handling uncooked food. If children are assisting in the preparation of any recipe, they should always be supervised by an adult.

The information in this book should not be used for diagnosing or treating any health problem. Not all diet and exercise plans suit everyone. You should always consult a trained medical professional before starting a diet, taking any form of medication, or embarking on any fitness or weight training program. The author and publisher disclaim any liability arising directly or indirectly from the use of this book.

Contains material adapted from the following titles published by Adams Media, an Imprint of Simon & Schuster, Inc.: The Everything® Air Fryer Cookbook by Michelle Fagone, copyright © 2018, ISBN 978-1-5072-0912-7, and The Everything® Low-Carb Meal Prep Cookbook by Lindsay Boyers, CHNC, copyright © 2018, ISBN 978-1-5072-0731-4.

NATIONAL LIBRARY OF AUSTRALIA
A catalogue record for this book is available from the National Library of Australia

ISBN: 9781761105746

Author: Michelle Fagone of CavegirlCuisine.com
Cover design: Meng Koach
Cover image: Lawrence Furzey
Internal photographs: James Stefiuk
Printed and bound in China by Leo Paper Products

FSC www.fsc.org MIX Paper from responsible sources FSC® C020056

Contents

To Samantha and Calla
You two have grown up to be such beautiful,
strong young women. I couldn't be prouder.
All my love, Mom

Introduction

If you have an air fryer, you probably already know that it is a revolutionary appliance that can save you time and help you live a healthier life. New to this amazing device? Well, you'll be excited to learn that you'll soon be using your air fryer to prepare nearly every meal, from breakfast and side dishes to dinner and dessert. What's so special about air frying, you ask?

The air fryer can replace your oven, microwave, deep fryer and dehydrator, and cook delicious meals in a fraction of the time you're used to. If you are looking to enjoy healthy meals but don't have a lot of time to spare, the air fryer is a game changer.

An air fryer can also help with your success on a low-carb diet. Typically, fried foods are filled with carbohydrates, so you might assume you have to avoid them altogether. With the air fryer, however, you still get the crunch of your favourite fried recipes — without the carbs. And you can choose your own low-carb batters and breadcrumbs! Another benefit to air frying is the short cooking times it provides. Long-term success on a low-carb diet is often attributed to ease of preparing healthy, diverse meals. That's why your air fryer will be your best friend throughout your low-carb journey and help you stay on track, even on those days when you are short on time — or patience.

In this book, you'll learn everything you need to know about using an air fryer, as well as some basics that will help you find success while eating a low-carb diet. You'll also find the perfect recipe for every occasion, from filling breakfasts, like BLT Frittata, to mouthwatering dinners for your whole family, such as Juicy Beef Sliders — and everything in between. So, let's get air frying!

1

Low-Carb Air Fryer Essentials

The air fryer is one of the most popular kitchen appliances for good reason: fried food can be made and enjoyed guilt-free! It also cooks foods quicker than your conventional oven, doesn't heat up your living space and is easy to clean. In this chapter, you will learn more about the functions of the air fryer and its handy accessories. You will also find further information on the low-carb diet, from what it really means to how it can impact your life for the better.

Keep in mind that while this chapter will cover the basics of using an air fryer, the first step is reading the manual that came with your air fryer. All air fryers are different, and there are a lot of different models on the market. Learning the ins and outs of your specific air fryer is the key to success, and it will familiarise you with troubleshooting issues as well as safety functions. Reading over the manual and washing all parts with warm, soapy water before the first use will get you ready to unleash your culinary finesse!

Why Own an Air Fryer?

The air fryer works by baking foods with a constant stream of circulating hot air that cooks food evenly and quickly, crisping up edges as it does its job. This is why the air fryer has quicker cooking times than a conventional oven — but the benefits of this appliance don't stop there. Here are a few more reasons to switch to air frying:

- **It replaces other cooking appliances.** Thanks to its quicker cooking times, the air fryer is the perfect alternative to your oven — but it can also replace your deep fryer, dehydrator and microwave! In one device, you'll be able to whip up perfect meals, snacks, sides and more without sacrificing any of the flavour.

- **It uses little to no cooking oil.** Traditionally cooked fried foods are prepared by submerging foods in heated oil, which means they are high in bad fats and calories. Also, when oil is heated beyond its smoking point, as with deep-frying, it can produce toxic fumes and free radicals. The air fryer drastically cuts down on fatty oils, meaning more nutritious meals. This can also lead to weight loss and better over-all health.

- **It makes vegetables appeal to the pickiest eaters.** A little low-carb breadcrumb and a fresh dipping sauce can turn zucchini into tasty fries. And a little ground pork rind breading on some cod can be the gateway recipe from fish fingers to a simple salmon fillet.

- **It reduces your energy bill.** When cooking casseroles or thicker cuts of meat, your traditional oven can provide a heat source that is not always welcomed, especially on those long, hot days. The contained heat of the air fryer will keep your air conditioner from working overtime.

Purchasing an Air Fryer

There are several brands, sizes and shapes of air fryers available. This book is based on a four-person 1,425-watt air fryer with a 2.8L capacity. Depending on your chosen model, the size of your food batches will vary, but cooking times will not be affected. For example, if you own a smaller two-person model, simply halve the ingredients in the chosen recipe. As for the temperature range, some air fryers allow you to dehydrate foods because you can cook them at a very low temperature for a long period of time. You'll want to make sure your air fryer has the appropriate cooking capacity and temperature range to meet your needs.

Air Fryer Functions

Settings can vary among different air fryer models on the market. Some of the newer types offer digital settings to control the temperature and time, while others have analog dials as well as preset temperatures for certain fresh and frozen foods. All recipes in this book were created using manual times and temperatures. Every air fryer allows you to set these yourself. Still, it is important to know how the cooking programs work on your air fryer and when to use them. And although some brands will claim you don't need to preheat the air fryer, skipping this step can alter cooking times. The recipes in this book include preheating instructions.

In addition, because the air fryer basket is going to be used when making most of your air-fried foods, finding a model with a quick-release button will make your life easier. This button releases the fryer basket containing food from the bottom basket so you can shake or flip the food with ease.

Air Fryer Accessories

The air fryer comes with a basic fryer basket; however, there are many other recipes that can be made with the purchase of a few accessories. Before you purchase any of these, make sure they work with your size and brand of air fryer. Here are some of the common air fryer accessories:

- **Metal holder.** This round metal rack allows for cooking a second layer of food in the air fryer.

- **Skewer rack.** This is similar to a metal holder but also contains four metal skewers for roasting meat and vegetable shish kebabs.

- **Ramekin.** Small ramekins are great for making mini cakes and quiches. If they're oven safe, they're safe to use in your air fryer.

- **Cake barrel.** You can purchase both round and square versions. A cake barrel is used for desserts, casseroles and egg dishes. As a bonus, both types of barrel have a handle, making retrieval from the air fryer a cinch.

- **Cupcake pan.** This pan usually comes with seven silicone cupcake liners (also called *baking cups*) that are oven safe and great for mini meatloaves, cupcakes, on-the-go frittatas, quick breads and muffins. They are reusable and dishwasher safe, making clean-up a snap!

- **Baking Paper.** Specially precut baking paper makes clean-up even easier when baking with your air fryer. You can also find baking paper with precut holes for steaming.

- **Pizza pan.** This is a shallow pan that allows you to make mini pizzas, as well as a variety of other recipes, such as biscuits, corn bread, Dutch pancakes and even the delectable Giant Chocolate Chip Cookie found on page 195.

- **Grill pan.** This replaces the air fryer basket and is used for grilling fish, meat and vegetables. Because there are no side walls, the pan allows for a bit more room than the air fryer basket.

Accessory Removal

When cooking pot-in-appliance, you'll want to be careful to avoid burning yourself once it's time to remove the inserted dish. Here are a couple useful tools for safely removing items from your air fryer:

- **Tongs.** Wooden or silicone-tipped tongs will help you remove pans that don't have handles, as well as flip food items, such as egg rolls and meat.

- **Oven mitts.** Heat-resistant mini mitts, or pinch mitts, are small food-grade silicone oven mitts that will help you lift pots out of the air fryer. They are more heat-resistant and less cumbersome than traditional oven mitts, which can prove to be bulky in the tight fryer basket.

- **Accessory removal hack.** You can also create an aluminium foil sling to lift a heated dish out of the air fryer. Simply fold a 25cm × 25cm square of aluminium foil in half, then fold again lengthwise. Place the sling underneath the bowl or pan before cooking.

Cleaning and Seasoning Your Air Fryer

After using your air fryer, unplug the appliance and allow it to completely cool. Adding cooler water to your fryer basket can cause warping. Although the removable parts are dishwasher safe, washing them by hand with warm, soapy water can lengthen the life of those coated nonstick parts.

To clean the air fryer pan you'll need to:

1. Remove the air fryer pan from the base. Fill the pan with hot water and dish soap. Let the pan soak with the frying basket inside for 10 minutes.
2. Clean the basket thoroughly with a sponge or brush.
3. Remove the fryer basket and scrub the underside and outside walls.
4. Clean the air fryer pan with a sponge or brush.
5. Let everything air-dry and return to the air fryer base.
6. Wipe the outside of the air fryer base with a damp cloth.

Once dry, the fryer basket can also be seasoned. You may have heard this term with cast-iron pans, but the air fryer basket can benefit from seasoning as well. Preheat the air fryer with the basket for 5 minutes at 200°C. Remove the basket and when cool enough to touch, spread a thin layer of coconut oil on the inside using a paper towel. Then simply heat the basket for an additional 2 minutes. This will help extend the life of the nonstick coating in the basket.

Breaking Down the Low-Carb Diet

Now that you have the basics of cooking with the air fryer down, it's time to take a look at the low-carb diet. What exactly does it mean? What foods are cut out or reduced? What is a net carb? Well, in the simplest terms, a low-carb diet means reducing the amount of carbohydrates you consume. Different low-carb diets have varying guidelines on how many carbohydrates, proteins and fats you should eat daily, but typically, a low-carb diet macronutrient breakdown looks something like this:

- Less than 20 percent of kilojoules from carbohydrates
- 25–30 percent of kilojoules from protein
- 50–55 percent of kilojoules from fat

Most low-carb diets eliminate the obvious sources of carbohydrates, like sugar, processed foods and desserts. Others also eliminate or reduce amounts of fruit and starchy vegetables like potatoes. There is no one-size-fits-all low-carb diet; it's up to you to find the balance of macronutrients and food choices that works for your body.

Total Carbs versus Net Carbs

When following a low-carb diet, you'll probably see or hear the term net carbs. The concept of net carbs is that certain carbohydrates affect your body in different ways, so you can count them differently when following a low-carb diet.

Refined sugars and starches — or carbohydrates that come from things like potatoes, white bread and sugar-laden desserts — are absorbed quickly into your bloodstream, causing a rapid spike in blood sugar and insulin, and affecting the way your body stores fat. On the other hand, complex carbohydrates — like the fibre from fruits and vegetables — move slowly through the digestive system and have little to no effect on blood sugar and insulin levels. In fact, some carbohydrates like insoluble fibre and sugar alcohols (erythritol and xylitol, to name two) move through the digestive system without entering your blood at all.

Based on this concept, some low-carb diets require you to count net carbohydrates instead of total carbohydrates. To calculate net carbohydrates, you'll simply subtract fibre and sugar alcohols from the total carbohydrate count. For example, if food contains 10 grams of total carbohydrates but 5 of those carbohydrates come from fibre and 1 comes from sugar alcohols, then the net carbs would be 4 grams.

The Benefits of a Low-Carb Diet

There are many reasons to go low-carb! Of course, weight loss is a big one, but low-carb diets offer significant health benefits beyond losing those pesky pounds. Check out the main benefits in the following list. When you understand the mechanisms of how something affects your body positively, you're more likely to stay on track:

- **Weight loss.** Low-carb diets help you shed extra pounds fairly quickly. This includes pounds from both excess water (short-term weight loss) and fat (long-term weight loss).

- **Better heart health.** Low-carb diets have been shown to improve all the significant markers for heart disease: low-density lipoprotein (or LDL), high-density lipoprotein (or HDL), triglycerides and blood pressure.

- **Reduced risk of metabolic syndrome.** Metabolic syndrome is a diagnosis given when a person has at least three of the following conditions at once: high blood pressure, high blood sugar, high levels of visceral fat, and abnormal cholesterol and triglyceride levels. Low-carb diets have been shown to dramatically improve every single marker associated with metabolic syndrome.

- **Better brain function.** Low-carb diets have shown promise for improving brain health and function. In one study, older adults who were considered at risk for developing Alzheimer's disease showed improvement in memory after following a low-carb diet for six weeks.

You've Got This!

You are ready to start air frying your own low-carb dishes, and this book is here to get you started. Make a meal plan during the weekend, then follow the simple and easy-to-make recipes for a week with far less stress. In most cases, a healthy dinner can take less than 30 minutes. So, have fun and happy eating!

2

Breakfast

Getting out the door on time is hard enough as it is — especially if you are juggling family as well. Fitting breakfast, not to mention one that is low-carb (most grab-and-go options out there seem to be carb-filled bars), into this hectic schedule can seem a bit overwhelming at times. Fortunately, the air fryer is here to save your morning, thanks to its shortened cooking time as well as the time you'll save by not having to stand over the frying pan.

This chapter offers a wide range of delicious, easy-to-make breakfast and brunch recipes for your air fryer, including Sugar-Free Bacon Strips, Egg Cups au Fromage and Cinnamon Breakfast Bread. And once you get comfortable with some of the basics, you should feel free to be creative and make some of your own morning masterpieces. So let your family wake up with a new appreciation for their soon-to-be-favourite kitchen appliance!

Grilled Grapefruit

Grilling a grapefruit helps bring some of the natural sugar to life, and the seasonings this recipe calls for cut some of that tartness that a raw grapefruit has. Don't forget to section the grapefruit before cooking, as it will help the toppings melt down into the crevices. Also, if you want to add a little flair, serve your grapefruit halves with fresh berries on top.

Hands-On Time: 5 minutes
Cook Time: 4 minutes

Serves 2

1 large grapefruit, cut in half
1 1/2 tablespoon erythritol sweetener
2 teaspoons ground cinnamon
1/8 teaspoon ground ginger
2 teaspoons butter, divided into 2 pats

1. Preheat air fryer at 200°C for 3 minutes.
2. Using a paring knife, cut each grapefruit section away from the inner membrane, keeping the sections remaining in the fruit.
3. In a small bowl, combine erythritol, cinnamon and ginger. Sprinkle over tops of grapefruit halves. Place 1 pat butter on top of each half.
4. Place grapefruit halves in ungreased air fryer basket and cook for 4 minutes.
5. Transfer to a medium serving plate and serve warm.

PER SERVING

KILOJOULES: 389 | **FAT:** 4g | **PROTEIN:** 1g | **SODIUM:** 1mg | **FIBRE:** 3g | **CARBOHYDRATES:** 22g | **NET CARBOHYDRATES:** 12g | **SUGAR:** 12g

Mexican-Style Sausage Balls

A perfect side dish for your breakfast table, these spicy and cheesy sausage balls are full of flavour. Enjoy with your favourite eggs and a bowl of fresh berries to round out the meal.

Hands-On Time: 10 minutes
Cook Time: 12 minutes

Serves 4

- 110 grams loose chorizo
- 340 grams pork sausage, removed from casing
- 1 ½ tablespoons canned green chiles, including juice
- 28 grams cream cheese, room temperature
- ¼ cup shredded Cheddar cheese

WHAT IS CHORIZO?

Chorizo is a spicy pork sausage often used in Spanish and Mexican cuisine. Spanish chorizo is traditionally dried and cured, while Mexican chorizo is encased and raw. In this recipe, cut the sausage from the casings or purchase loose.

1. Preheat air fryer at 200°C for 3 minutes.
2. In a large bowl, combine all ingredients. Form mixture into 16 x 3cm balls. Place sausage balls in ungreased air fryer basket.
3. Cook for 6 minutes, then shake basket and cook for an additional 6 minutes until a meat thermometer ensures an internal temperature of at least 75°C.
4. Transfer to a large serving plate and serve warm.

PER SERVING

KILOJOULES: 1259 | **FAT:** 23g | **PROTEIN:** 21g | **SODIUM:** 388mg | **FIBRE:** 0g | **CARBOHYDRATES:** 1g | **NET CARBOHYDRATES:** 1g | **SUGAR:** 0g

Air-Fried Hard-"Boiled" Eggs

The air fryer provides a super-easy method for hard-boiling eggs. These Air-Fried Hard-"Boiled" Eggs are a perfect protein and can be enjoyed wholly as a snack, sliced into salads or transformed into deviled eggs.

Hands-On Time: 5 minutes
Cook Time: 15 minutes

Serves 8

8 large eggs
1 cup ice cubes
2 cups water

1 Preheat air fryer at 120°C for 3 minutes.

2 Add eggs to ungreased air fryer basket. Cook for 15 minutes.

3 Add ice and water to a large bowl. Transfer cooked eggs to this water bath immediately to stop cooking process. After 5 minutes, peel eggs and serve.

PER SERVING

KILOJOULES: 297 | **FAT:** 5g | **PROTEIN:** 6g | **SODIUM:** 71mg | **FIBRE:** 0g | **CARBOHYDRATES:** 0g | **NET CARBOHYDRATES:** 0g | **SUGAR:** 0g

Sugar-Free Bacon Strips

Sugar-free bacon is available at specialty stores and online; however, if you cannot find any in your region, try a fatty middle bacon variety. All bacon will contain sugar due to the curing process — read the ingredient list on the packet and select one with a low sugar content.

Hands-On Time: 5 minutes
Cook Time: 12 minutes

Serves 4

1 ½ tablespoons water
8 sugar-free bacon, halved

1 Preheat air fryer at 200°C for 3 minutes.

2 Pour water into bottom of air fryer to ensure minimum smoke from fat drippings. Place half of bacon in ungreased air fryer basket and cook for 3 minutes. Flip, then cook for an additional 3 minutes.

3 Transfer cooked bacon to a medium paper towel-lined serving plate and repeat cooking with remaining bacon. Serve warm.

PER SERVING

KILOJOULES: 251 | **FAT:** 5g | **PROTEIN:** 4g | **SODIUM:** 290mg | **FIBRE:** 0g | **CARBOHYDRATES:** 0g | **NET CARBOHYDRATES:** 0g | **SUGAR:** 0g

Scotch Eggs

Although this treat is traditionally enjoyed as pub food, breakfast is a perfect time of day for it. C'mon: sausage and eggs — that are portable! If you prefer a runnier yolk, under cook the hard-boiled eggs by a few minutes before preparing the dish.

Hands-On Time: 10 minutes
Cook Time: 14 minutes

Serves 4

- 450 grams pork sausage, removed from casing
- 2 teaspoons Dijon mustard
- 2 teaspoons peeled and grated brown onion
- 3/4 tablespoon chopped fresh chives
- 3/4 tablespoon chopped fresh parsley
- 1/8 teaspoon ground nutmeg
- 1/2 teaspoon salt
- 1/4 teaspoon freshly ground black pepper
- 4 large hard-boiled eggs, peeled
- 1 large egg, beaten
- 1 cup crushed pork rinds
- 2 teaspoons olive oil

1. Preheat air fryer at 180°C for 3 minutes.
2. Combine sausage, mustard, onion, chives, parsley, nutmeg, salt and pepper in a large bowl. Separate mixture into four even balls.
3. Form sausage balls evenly around hard-boiled eggs, then dip in beaten egg and cover in pork rinds.
4. Place sausage balls in air fryer basket lightly greased with olive oil. Cook for 7 minutes, then gently turn and brush lightly with olive oil. Cook for an additional 7 minutes.
5. Transfer to a large serving plate and serve warm.

PER SERVING

KILOJOULES: 1681 | **FAT:** 28g | **PROTEIN:** 34g | **SODIUM:** 635mg | **FIBRE:** 0g | **CARBOHYDRATES:** 1g | **NET CARBOHYDRATES:** 1g | **SUGAR:** 1g

Bacon Vegetable Morning Hash

To round out this savoury breakfast hash, serve it with an egg on top. Poached or over-medium eggs are great, as the runny yolk acts as a sauce for the dish. But if you are in a hurry, just scramble an egg and add it to your bowl. And if you are feeling a little cheesy, throw in some grated Cheddar cheese!

Hands-On Time: 10 minutes
Cook Time: 12 minutes

Serves 4

- **25 small Brussels sprouts, halved**
- **2 mini sweet capsicum, seeded and diced**
- **1 small brown onion, peeled and diced**
- **3 slices sugar-free bacon, diced**
- **2 tablespoons fresh orange juice**
- **¼ teaspoon salt**
- **1 teaspoon orange zest**

1. Preheat air fryer at 180°C for 3 minutes.
2. In a medium bowl, combine all ingredients except orange zest.
3. Add mixture to ungreased air fryer basket. Cook for 6 minutes, then toss and cook for an additional 6 minutes. Serve warm.

PER SERVING

KILOJOULES: 343 | **FAT:** 2g | **PROTEIN:** 6g | **SODIUM:** 285mg | **FIBRE:** 5g | **CARBOHYDRATES:** 14g | **NET CARBOHYDRATES:** 9g | **SUGAR:** 4g

SPICE IT UP

If you're feeling spicy, swap the mini sweet capsicums for a poblano or jalapeño chilli. It will be sure to start your morning with a kick!

Creamy Herbed Scrambled Eggs

When your scrambled eggs need an extra boost, a little sour cream and goat cheese takes breakfast to the next level. The parsley also adds colour and helps brighten the other flavours of the dish.

Hands-On Time: 5 minutes
Cook Time: 7 minutes

Serves 2

4 large eggs
1/4 teaspoon salt
1/8 teaspoon freshly ground black pepper
2 teaspoons sour cream
3/4 tablespoon goat cheese crumbled
3/4 tablespoon chopped fresh parsley, divided

1. Preheat air fryer at 200°C for 3 minutes.
2. In a small bowl, whisk together eggs, salt and pepper.
3. Add egg mixture to a cake barrel lightly greased with olive oil. Add barrel to air fryer basket and cook for 5 minutes.
4. Remove cake barrel from air fryer and use a silicone spatula to stir eggs. Add sour cream, goat cheese and half of parsley. Place barrel back in air fryer and cook for an additional 2 minutes.
5. Transfer eggs to a medium serving dish and garnish with remaining parsley. Serve warm.

PER SERVING

KILOJOULES: 699 | **FAT:** 12g | **PROTEIN:** 14g | **SODIUM:** 454mg | **FIBRE:** 0g | **CARBOHYDRATES:** 1g | **NET CARBOHYDRATES:** 1g | **SUGAR:** 1g

Maple Sage Breakfast Sausages

The maple syrup lends a sweetness against the savoury spices and the pine-like flavour of the sage. And these links are void of any preservatives and fillers that store-bought counterparts may be filled with.

Hands-On Time: 10 minutes
Cook Time: 9 minutes

Makes 8 sausages

- **340 grams mild pork sausage, removed from casings**
- **1 teaspoon rubbed sage**
- **1 ½ tablespoons pure maple syrup**
- **⅛ teaspoon cayenne pepper**
- **¼ teaspoon salt**
- **¼ teaspoon freshly ground black pepper**
- **¾ tablespoon water**

1. Preheat air fryer at 200°C for 3 minutes.
2. Combine pork, sage, maple syrup, cayenne pepper, salt and black pepper. Form into eight sausages.
3. Pour water into bottom of air fryer. Place links in air fryer basket. Cook for 9 minutes.
4. Transfer to a plate and serve warm.

PER SERVING (1 SAUSAGE LINK)

KILOJOULES: 386 | **FAT:** 6g | **PROTEIN:** 4g | **SODIUM:** 234mg | **FIBRE:** 0g | **CARBOHYDRATES:** 4g | **NET CARBOHYDRATES:** 4g | **SUGAR:** 3g

Brunchy Shakshuka Capsicum Cups

Shakshuka is a Middle Eastern dish that is perfect not only for brunch but also any time of the day. Traditionally, the main ingredients are served in a sauce that contains diced capsicums, but we've flipped the script in this recipe by putting the ingredients in the capsicum, making each a personal little gift! Use a variety of capsicum colours for a more whimsical presentation.

Hands-On Time: 10 minutes
Cook Time: 22 minutes

Serves 4

- **3/4 tablespoon olive oil**
- **1/2 medium brown onion, peeled and diced**
- **2 cloves garlic, peeled and minced**
- **1 (1cm) knob turmeric, peeled and minced**
- **410 grams canned diced tomatoes, including juice**
- **3/4 tablespoon no-added-sugar tomato paste**
- **1/2 teaspoon smoked paprika**
- **1/2 teaspoon salt**
- **1/2 teaspoon erythritol sweetener**
- **1/4 teaspoon ground cumin**
- **1/4 teaspoon ground coriander**
- **1/8 teaspoon cayenne pepper**
- **4 small capsicums, any colour, tops removed and seeded**
- **4 large eggs**
- **1 1/2 tablespoons fetta cheese crumbled**
- **1 1/2 tablespoons chopped fresh parsley**

1. In a medium saucepan, heat olive oil over medium heat for 30 seconds. Add onion and stir-fry for 10 minutes until softened.
2. Add garlic and turmeric to pan and heat another minute. Add diced tomatoes, tomato paste, paprika, salt, erythritol, cumin, coriander and cayenne pepper. Remove from heat and stir.
3. Preheat air fryer at 180°C for 3 minutes.
4. Place capsicum in ungreased air fryer basket. Divide tomato mixture among capsicum. Crack one egg onto tomato mixture in each capsicum.
5. Cook for 9 minutes, then remove from air fryer and sprinkle fetta cheese on top of eggs. Place back in air fryer and cook for 1 minute.
6. Remove from air fryer and let rest for 5 minutes on a large serving plate. Garnish with parsley and serve warm.

PER SERVING

KILJOULES: 707 | **FAT:** 10g | **PROTEIN:** 9g | **SODIUM:** 519mg | **FIBRE:** 3g | **CARBOHYDRATES:** 12g | **NET CARBOHYDRATES:** 8g | **SUGAR:** 6g

Egg Cups au Fromage

These quick, easy and portable eggs cups are a riff on the traditional French dish Quiche au Fromage. They have all of the wonderful flavour, with none of the carbs! As a money saver, Swiss cheese can be used instead of Gruyère, thanks to the similar flavour profiles of both cheeses.

Hands-On Time: 10 minutes
Cook Time: 18 minutes

Serves 6

- **4 large eggs**
- **1 1/2 tablespoons thickened cream**
- **1/8 teaspoon salt**
- **1/8 teaspoon freshly ground black pepper**
- **1/8 teaspoon ground nutmeg**
- **1/4 cup shredded Gruyère cheese**

1. Preheat air fryer at 180°C for 3 minutes. Lightly grease six silicone muffin cups with olive oil.
2. In a small bowl, whisk together eggs, heavy cream, salt, pepper and nutmeg. Stir in Gruyère cheese.
3. Distribute egg mixture into prepared muffin cups. Place three cups in air fryer basket and cook for 9 minutes.
4. Transfer cooked cups to a large serving plate to cool and repeat cooking with remaining cups. Serve warm.

PER SERVING

KILOJOULES: 347 | **FAT:** 6g | **PROTEIN:** 6g | **SODIUM:** 106mg | **FIBRE:** 0g | **CARBOHYDRATES:** 0g | **NET CARBOHYDRATES:** 0g | **SUGAR:** 0g

Buffalo Chicken Egg Cups

This dish is a great way to utilise any leftover chicken. Plus, because it is cooked in muffin cups, it's a perfect grab-and-go breakfast!

Hands-On Time: 10 minutes
Cook Time: 18 minutes

Serves 6

- **3 large eggs**
- **1 ½ tablespoons thickened cream**
- **4 teaspoons buffalo wing sauce**
- **¼ cup shredded Cheddar cheese**
- **¼ cup shredded cooked chicken breast**

1. Preheat air fryer at 180°C for 3 minutes. Lightly grease six silicone muffin cups with olive oil.
2. In a medium bowl, whisk together eggs, thickened cream and buffalo wing sauce. Stir in Cheddar cheese and chicken.
3. Distribute egg mixture into prepared muffin cups. Place three cups in air fryer basket and cook for 9 minutes.
4. Transfer cooked cups to a large serving plate to cool and repeat cooking with remaining cups. Serve warm.

PER SERVING

KILOJOULES: 343 | **FAT:** 6g | **PROTEIN:** 6g | **SODIUM:** 174mg | **FIBRE:** 0g | **CARBOHYDRATES:** 1g | **NET CARBOHYDRATES:** 0g | **SUGAR:** 0g

Morning Egg Cups

Bacon, cheese and eggs: the breakfast trifecta! Add a little cream, salt and pepper, and you have a meal that pleases almost everyone. Add diced onion and capsicum for a sweet crunch.

Hands-On Time: 10 minutes
Cook Time: 18 minutes

Serves 6

- **3 large eggs**
- **1 1/2 tablespoons thickened cream**
- **1/8 teaspoon salt**
- **1/8 teaspoon freshly ground black pepper**
- **3 cooked sugar-free bacon slices, diced**
- **1/4 cup shredded Cheddar cheese**

1. Preheat air fryer at 180°C for 3 minutes. Lightly grease six silicone muffin cups with olive oil.
2. In a small bowl, whisk together eggs, thickened cream, salt and pepper. Stir in bacon and Cheddar cheese.
3. Distribute egg mixture into prepared muffin cups. Place three cups in air fryer basket and cook for 9 minutes.
4. Transfer cooked cups to a large serving plate and repeat cooking with remaining cups. Serve warm.

PER SERVING

KILOJOULES: 345 | **FAT:** 7g | **PROTEIN:** 5g | **SODIUM:** 189mg | **FIBRE:** 0g | **CARBOHYDRATES:** 0g | **NET CARBOHYDRATES:** 0g | **SUGAR:** 0g

BLT Frittata

This dish is hearty enough for a brunch and perfect for replenishing your energy after a morning exercise routine. You get all of the flavours of a BLT without the guilt of the grain!

Hands-On Time: 10 minutes
Cook Time: 14 minutes

Serves 2

- 5 large eggs
- 1/4 teaspoon salt
- 1/4 teaspoon freshly ground black pepper
- 4 slices cooked sugar-free bacon, diced
- 1/2 cup grated Cheddar cheese
- 1 large Roma tomato, cored and sliced
- 1 cup shredded iceberg lettuce
- 1 1/2 tablespoons sour cream

1. Preheat air fryer at 160°C for 3 minutes.
2. In a medium bowl, whisk together eggs, salt and pepper. Stir in bacon and Cheddar cheese. Pour mixture into a cake barrel lightly greased with olive oil. Place tomato slices on top.
3. Place barrel in air fryer basket and cook for 14 minutes.
4. Transfer cake barrel to a cooling rack to cool for 5 minutes, then slice frittata and serve warm topped with lettuce and sour cream.

PER SERVING

KILOJOULES: 1656 | **FAT:** 29g | **PROTEIN:** 27g | **SODIUM:** 956mg | **FIBRE:** 1g | **CARBOHYDRATES:** 6g | **NET CARBOHYDRATES:** 5g | **SUGAR:** 4g

Tomato and Spinach Frittata

Serve this light and tasty frittata on one of those lazy weekend mornings. Pour yourself a mimosa, find a series you've been meaning to watch and crawl right back under the covers to enjoy your special breakfast in bed.

Hands-On Time: 10 minutes
Cook Time: 14 minutes

Serves 4

- 5 large eggs
- 1/4 teaspoon salt
- 1/4 teaspoon freshly ground black pepper
- 1/2 cup fresh baby spinach leaves
- 1 large spring onion, peeled and diced
- 110 grams goat cheese crumbled
- 1 large Roma tomato, cored and sliced

1. Preheat air fryer at 160°C for 3 minutes.
2. In a medium bowl, whisk together eggs, salt and pepper. Stir in spinach, shallot and goat cheese. Pour mixture into a cake barrel lightly greased with olive oil. Place tomato slices on top.
3. Place barrel in air fryer basket and cook for 14 minutes.
4. Transfer to a cooling rack to cool for 5 minutes in cake barrel, then slice and serve warm.

PER SERVING

KILOJOULES: 866 | **FAT:** 14g | **PROTEIN:** 15g | **SODIUM:** 362mg | **FIBRE:** 1g | **CARBOHYDRATES:** 4g | **NET CARBOHYDRATES:** 3g | **SUGAR:** 2g

Fiesta Breakfast Casserole

Loaded with flavour, this casserole will have your taste buds doing a little dance. Not only is it a tasty breakfast, but it could even be used as a Taco Tuesday meal, with the green chillies and avocado helping make your case. But do you really need an excuse to eat breakfast for dinner?

Hands-On Time: 10 minutes
Cook Time: 14 minutes

Serves 2

- 5 large eggs
- 1 ½ tablespoons thickened cream
- ½ teaspoon ground cumin
- ¼ teaspoon salt
- ¼ teaspoon freshly ground black pepper
- ¼ cup loose cooked spicy breakfast sausage
- ½ cup Mexican blend cheese
- 1 large Roma tomato, cored, seeded and diced
- 130 grams canned green chillies, including juice
- 1 small avocado, peeled, pitted and diced

1. Preheat air fryer at 160°C for 3 minutes.
2. In a medium bowl, whisk together eggs, thickened cream, cumin, salt and pepper. Stir in sausage, Mexican blend cheese, tomato, chillies and avocado. Pour mixture into a cake barrel lightly greased with olive oil.
3. Place barrel in air fryer basket and cook for 14 minutes.
4. Transfer barrel to a cooling rack to cool for 5 minutes, then slice and serve warm.

PER SERVING

KILOJOULES: 2384 | **FAT:** 44g | **PROTEIN:** 28g | **SODIUM:** 1,397mg | **FIBRE:** 9g | **CARBOHYDRATES:** 18g | **NET CARBOHYDRATES:** 9g | **SUGAR:** 5g

Cinnamon Pecan Crunch Cereal

Sometimes low-carb breakfasts can feel a little repetitive with all of the egg dishes when you just want a bowl of cereal. Well, now you can make your own grain-free version! Serve with some unsweetened almond milk or over a bowl of Greek yoghurt with fresh berries.

Hands-On Time: 5 minutes
Cook Time: 6 minutes

Serves 4

- 1 cup pecan pieces
- 1 cup unsalted sunflower seeds
- 1 cup unsweetened coconut flakes
- ¼ cup erythritol sweetener
- ⅛ cup coconut flour
- ⅛ cup pecan flour
- 2 teaspoons ground cinnamon
- 1½ tablespoons melted butter
- 1½ tablespoons raw almond butter
- ⅛ teaspoon salt

1. Preheat air fryer at 150°C for 3 minutes.
2. Combine all ingredients in a medium bowl.
3. Spoon mixture into an ungreased round 4-cup baking dish. Place in air fryer basket and cook for 3 minutes. Stir, then cook for an additional 3 minutes.
4. Transfer to an airtight container, let cool for 10 minutes, then cover and store at room temperature until ready to serve.

PER SERVING

KILOJOULES: 2702 | **FAT:** 61g | **PROTEIN:** 13g | **SODIUM:** 107mg | **FIBRE:** 13g | **CARBOHYDRATES:** 33g | **NET CARBOHYDRATES:** 9g | **SUGAR:** 4g

WHERE DO I FIND PECAN FLOUR?

Usually, almond flour is the most readily available nut flour on the market, and although sold commercially, nut flours can be a little pricey. But I'll share a secret with you: the only ingredient you need is your choice of nut. Just throw a handful in the food processor and pulse to your desired consistency, whether chunky or fine, depending on the recipe. But don't pulse for too long, as you'll create a nut butter!

Vanilla Nut Granola

Serve this addictive granola as a cereal with your favourite milk, as a trail mix snack or over Greek yoghurt.

Hands-On Time: 5 minutes
Cook Time: 6 minutes

Serves 4

- ½ cup slivered almonds
- ½ cup pecan pieces
- ½ cup unsalted sunflower seeds
- ½ cup pumpkin seeds
- 1 cup unsweetened coconut flakes
- ¼ cup erythritol sweetener
- ⅛ cup coconut flour
- ⅛ cup almond flour
- 1 teaspoon vanilla extract
- 1 ½ tablespoons melted butter
- 1 ½ tablespoons raw almond butter
- ⅛ teaspoon salt

1. Preheat air fryer at 150°C for 3 minutes.
2. Combine all ingredients in a medium bowl.
3. Spoon mixture into an ungreased round 4-cup oven-safe baking dish and place in air fryer basket. Cook for 3 minutes, then stir and cook for an additional 3 minutes.
4. Transfer to an airtight container and cool for 10 minutes, then cover and store at room temperature until ready to serve.

PER SERVING

KILOJOULES: 2564 | **FAT:** 57g | **PROTEIN:** 16g | **SODIUM:** 109mg | **FIBRE:** 11g | **CARBOHYDRATES:** 31g | **NET CARBOHYDRATES:** 8g | **SUGAR:** 4g

Cinnamon Breakfast Bread

If you are missing that good ol' stack of pancakes in the morning, this breakfast bread will be your new favourite. Serve topped with butter, sugar-free syrup, fresh berries or all of the above!

Hands-On Time: 5 minutes
Cook Time: 10 minutes

Serves 2

- **½ cup finely ground almond flour**
- **¼ cup powdered erythritol sweetener**
- **½ teaspoon baking powder**
- **⅛ teaspoon salt**
- **1 ½ tablespoons butter, melted**
- **1 large egg**
- **½ teaspoon unflavoured gelatin**
- **½ teaspoon vanilla extract**
- **½ teaspoon ground cinnamon**

1. Preheat air fryer at 150°C for 3 minutes.
2. In a medium bowl, combine flour, erythritol, baking powder and salt. Set aside.
3. In a small bowl, combine butter, egg, gelatin, vanilla and cinnamon. Add egg mixture to flour mixture and stir until smooth.
4. Spoon mixture into an ungreased pizza pan. Place pan in air fryer basket and cook for 10 minutes.
5. Remove pan and let set for 5 minutes, then slice and serve warm.

PER SERVING

KILOJOULES: 1276 | **FAT:** 28g | **PROTEIN:** 10g | **SODIUM:** 284mg | **FIBRE:** 3g | **CARBOHYDRATES:** 31g | **NET CARBOHYDRATES:** 4g | **SUGAR:** 1g

Pecan Streusel Coffee Cake

A sweet bite to enjoy with a cup of coffee or tea, this cake is layered to perfection. A little is all you'll need. It consists of cake and a cinnamon layer topped with a creamy cheesecake and pecan streusel. Don't let the long ingredient list scare you away — a lot of the ingredients are repeated in each layer.

Hands-On Time: 5 minutes
Cook Time: 15 minutes

Serves 8

For Cake
- 1/2 cup finely ground almond flour
- 1/4 cup erythritol sweetener
- 1/2 teaspoon baking powder
- 1/2 teaspoon instant espresso powder
- 1/8 teaspoon salt
- 1 1/2 tablespoons butter, melted
- 1 large egg
- 1/2 teaspoon cream of tartar
- 1/2 teaspoon vanilla extract
- 1/2 teaspoon ground cinnamon

For Cinnamon Layer
- 2 1/4 tablespoons butter, melted
- 1/3 cup erythritol sweetener
- 1 tablespoon ground cinnamon
- 1 1/2 tablespoons cassava flour

For Cheesecake
- 170 grams cream cheese, room temperature
- 1 1/2 tablespoons erythritol sweetener
- 1/4 teaspoon vanilla extract
- 1 large egg

For Pecan Streusel
- 1/3 cup pecan pieces
- 1/4 teaspoon ground cinnamon
- 1/4 teaspoon vanilla extract
- 1/4 cup erythritol sweetener
- 1 1/2 tablespoons butter, melted

1. **To make Cake:** In a medium bowl, combine all ingredients. Spread in a 18cm springform pan greased with cooking spray.
2. **To make Cinnamon Layer:** In a small bowl, combine all ingredients. Spread over cake in pan.
3. **To make Cheesecake:** In a medium bowl, combine all ingredients until smooth. Spread over cinnamon layer.
4. **To make Pecan Streusel:** In a small bowl, combine all ingredients. Drop in small crumbles over cheesecake.
5. Preheat air fryer at 150°C for 3 minutes. Cover pan with aluminium foil.
6. Place pan in air fryer basket and cook for 10 minutes. Remove foil and cook for an additional 5 minutes.
7. Let pan cool for 30 minutes uncovered, then cover and refrigerate for at least 2 hours, up to overnight. Slice and serve.

PER SERVING

KILOJOULES: 1113 | **FAT:** 25g | **PROTEIN:** 5g | **SODIUM:** 148mg | **FIBRE:** 2g | **CARBOHYDRATES:** 29g | **NET CARBOHYDRATES:** 5g | **SUGAR:** 1g

Pumpkin Nut Muffins

Yes, you can still have muffins on a low-carb diet! When that sweet tooth is calling, this is an excellent recipe for staying true to your low-carb regime.

Hands-On Time: 10 minutes
Cook Time: 7 minutes

Serves 6

- **1/2 cup almond flour**
- **1/2 cup erythritol sweetener**
- **1/2 teaspoon baking powder**
- **1/4 teaspoon pumpkin pie spice (see page 209)**
- **1/8 teaspoon ground nutmeg**
- **1/8 teaspoon salt**
- **1/4 cup pumpkin purée**
- **1/4 teaspoon vanilla extract**
- **2 1/4 tablespoons butter, melted**
- **2 large eggs**
- **1/4 cup crushed walnuts**

ROAST PUMPKIN PUREE

A roasted pumpkin puree will provide a richer flavour and it's easy to make. Simply cut a medium to small pumpkin in half. Scrape out the seeds and place halves, cut side down on a lined baking tray. Heat oven to 180°C and roast for one-and-a-half hours or until a fork can easily pierce them. Cool the pumpkin havles, scoop the pulp out and puree in a blender.

1. Preheat air fryer at 190°C for 3 minutes.
2. In a large bowl, combine flour, erythritol, baking powder, pumpkin pie spice, nutmeg and salt. Set aside.
3. In a medium bowl, combine pumpkin purée, vanilla, butter and eggs. Pour wet ingredients into bowl with dry ingredients and gently combine.
4. Add walnuts to batter. Do not overmix. Spoon batter into six silicone cupcake liners lightly greased with olive oil.
5. Place cupcake liners in air fryer basket and cook for 7 minutes.
6. Transfer muffins in silicone liners to a cooling rack to cool for 5 minutes, then serve.

PER SERVING

KILOJOULES: 673 | **FAT:** 15g | **PROTEIN:** 5g | **SODIUM:** 107mg | **FIBRE:** 1g | **CARBOHYDRATES:** 19g | **NET CARBOHYDRATES:** 2g | **SUGAR:** 1g

Strawberry Basil Muffins

Strawberries and basil are a terrific combination, and even better in the form of this tasty breakfast treat. It's perfect for a warm-weather morning — or any morning, really.

Hands-On Time: 10 minutes
Cook Time: 7 minutes

Serves 6

- **1/4 cup almond flour**
- **1/4 cup coconut flour**
- **1/2 cup erythritol sweetener**
- **1/2 teaspoon baking powder**
- **1/8 teaspoon salt**
- **1/2 cup hulled and finely chopped fresh strawberries**
- **1/4 teaspoon vanilla extract**
- **2 1/4 tablespoons butter, melted**
- **2 large eggs**
- **3/4 tablespoon chopped fresh basil**

1. Preheat air fryer at 190°C for 3 minutes.
2. In a large bowl, combine almond flour, coconut flour, erythritol, baking powder and salt. Set aside.
3. In a medium bowl, combine strawberries, vanilla, butter and eggs. Pour wet ingredients into large bowl with dry ingredients. Gently combine.
4. Add basil to batter. Do not over mix. Spoon batter into six silicone cupcake liners lightly greased with olive oil.
5. Place liners in air fryer basket and cook for 7 minutes.
6. Transfer muffins in silicone liners to a cooling rack to cool for 5 minutes, then serve.

PER SERVING

KILJOULES: 531 | **FAT:** 10g | **PROTEIN:** 4g | **SODIUM:** 115mg | **FIBRE:** 2g | **CARBOHYDRATES:** 21g | **NET CARBOHYDRATES:** 3g | **SUGAR:** 1g

3

Appetisers, Snacks and Sauces

Living within certain diet requirements is never harder than when you are with a group of friends. Chips and dips and deep-fried, crumbed everything seem to swarm the tables. But boring plates of unhealthy food don't have to be your fate — bring a healthy, delicious low-carb option to share. Better yet, throw your own shindig and show everyone what they've been missing! Tasty appetisers and snacks are a great way to bring a group of people together to enjoy a sports game or tide them over until you serve a meal.

Quick, crispy food air-fried in minutes? Now that's how you throw a party! With amazing appetisers and snacks ranging from Chicken Enchilada Dip and Chipotle Avocado Fries to California Roll Deviled Eggs and Eggplant Parmie Sticks — paired with delectable sauces like Low-Carb Honey Mustard — the only problem you'll have incorporating the recipes in this chapter into your next social event will be deciding which ones to make. Your guests won't even know they are eating low-carb recipes!

Hot Reuben Dip

This recipe takes the traditional Reuben sandwich flavours and combines them into one seriously addictive dip. Serve with your favourite vegetables for dipping.

Hands-On Time: 10 minutes
Cook Time: 10 minutes

Serves 6

- 230 grams cream cheese, room temperature
- 1/4 cup mayonnaise
- 1/4 cup sour cream
- 1 cup chopped deli corned beef
- 1 cup drained sauerkraut
- 1 cup shredded Swiss cheese, divided
- 1 teaspoon caraway seeds

1. Preheat air fryer to 200°C for 3 minutes.
2. In a large bowl, mix cream cheese, mayonnaise and sour cream until combined. Add corned beef, sauerkraut, 1/2 cup Swiss cheese and caraway seeds.
3. Spoon mixture into an ungreased 15cm oven-safe baking dish. Sprinkle remaining cheese on top.
4. Place dish in air fryer basket. Cook for 10 minutes.
5. Serve warm.

PER SERVING

KILOJOULES: 1338 | **FAT:** 29g | **PROTEIN:** 13g | **SODIUM:** 583mg | **FIBRE:** 1g | **CARBOHYDRATES:** 4g | **NET CARBOHYDRATES:** 4g | **SUGAR:** 2g

Baked Garlic Ricotta

This has all of the richness and creaminess of a soufflé but is much more forgiving. Serve with vegetables, alongside your favourite protein or even as an accompaniment to a charcuterie tray.

Hands-On Time: 10 minutes
Cook Time: 7 minutes

Serves 4

- **2 cloves peeled Simple Roasted Garlic (see recipe on page 79)**
- **1 1/2 cups ricotta cheese**
- **1/2 cup grated Parmesan cheese**
- **1 large egg, beaten**
- **3/4 tablespoon olive oil**
- **3/4 tablespoon fresh lemon juice**
- **1/4 teaspoon salt**
- **1/4 teaspoon freshly ground black pepper**
- **1 teaspoon finely chopped fresh rosemary**

1. Preheat air fryer to 180°C for 3 minutes.
2. Squeeze garlic into a medium bowl. Using the back of a fork, mash until a garlic paste is formed. Add remaining ingredients and combine.
3. Spoon mixture into an ungreased 15cm oven-safe baking dish.
4. Place dish in air fryer basket. Cook for 7 minutes.
5. Serve warm.

PER SERVING

KILOJOULES: 1075 | **FAT:** 16g | **PROTEIN:** 16g | **SODIUM:** 411mg | **FIBRE:** 0g | **CARBOHYDRATES:** 5g | **NET CARBOHYDRATES:** 5g | **SUGAR:** 1g

Mediterranean Jalapeño Poppers

Kalamata olives + fetta cheese + mint leaves = a traditional, tasty combination. Add a little pork and stuff it into jalapeño halves and you've just taken this bar food up a notch! And if you prefer more heat, instead of discarding the jalapeño seeds, simply fold them into the cheese mixture.

Hands-On Time: 10 minutes
Cook Time: 18 minutes

Serves 6

- 1 tablespoon olive oil
- 110 grams pork mince
- 1 ½ tablespoons pitted and finely diced kalamata olives
- 1 ½ tablespoons fetta cheese
- 28 grams cream cheese, room temperature
- ½ teaspoon dried mint leaves
- 6 large jalapeños, sliced in half lengthwise and seeded

1. In a medium frying pan, heat olive oil over medium-high heat 30 seconds. Add pork and cook for 6 minutes until no longer pink. Drain fat.
2. Preheat air fryer to 180°C for 3 minutes.
3. In a medium bowl, combine cooked pork, olives, fetta cheese, cream cheese and mint leaves.
4. Press pork mixture into peppers.
5. Place half of poppers in ungreased air fryer basket. Cook for 6 minutes. Transfer to a medium serving plate and repeat cooking with remaining poppers.
6. Serve warm.

PER SERVING

KILOJOULES: 485 | **FAT:** 10g | **PROTEIN:** 6g | **SODIUM:** 125mg | **FIBRE:** 0g | **CARBOHYDRATES:** 2g | **NET CARBOHYDRATES:** 1g | **SUGAR:** 1g

Baked Brie with Orange Marmalade and Spiced Walnuts

Whether you are entertaining your wine group or workout buddies, or just lunchin' with your besties, this elegant appetiser will please all. Serve with vegetables — or even a mix of vegetables and crackers for your carb-loving guests. Just be sure to send those leftover crackers home with someone else so you aren't tempted later!

Hands-On Time: 10 minutes
Cook Time: 22 minutes

Serves 6

- **1 cup walnuts**
- **1 large egg white, beaten**
- **1/8 teaspoon ground cumin**
- **1/8 teaspoon cayenne pepper**
- **1 teaspoon ground cinnamon**
- **1/4 teaspoon powdered erythritol**
- **1 round Brie (230 grams)**
- **1 1/2 tablespoons reduced sugar orange marmalade**

1. Preheat air fryer at 160°C for 3 minutes.
2. Combine walnuts with egg white in a small bowl. Set aside.
3. In a separate small bowl, combine cumin, cayenne pepper, cinnamon and erythritol. Add walnuts, drained of excess egg white, and toss.
4. Place walnuts in ungreased air fryer basket. Cook for 6 minutes, then toss nuts and cook for an additional 6 minutes.
5. Transfer to a small bowl and let cool for about 5 minutes until easy to handle. When cooled, chop into smaller bits.
6. Adjust air fryer temperature to 200°C. Place Brie in an ungreased pizza pan or on a piece of baking paper cut to size of air fryer basket. Cook for 10 minutes.
7. Transfer Brie to a medium serving plate and garnish with orange marmalade and spiced walnuts.

PER SERVING

KILOJOULESS: 1167 | **FAT:** 24g | **PROTEIN:** 12g | **SODIUM:** 250mg | **FIBRE:** 2g | **CARBOHYDRATES:** 8g| **NET CARBOHYDRATES:** 2g | **SUGAR:** 1g

Pepperoni Pizza Bread

This snack is after-school perfection! There is no need to heat up those nutrient-lacking frozen pizzas when you can make this easy-peasy pepperoni pizza bread instead. Slice into strips and dip in a warmed napolitana sauce.

Hands-On Time: 5 minutes
Cook Time: 20 minutes

Serves 4

2 large eggs, beaten
1 ½ tablespoons coconut flour
1 ½ tablespoons cassava flour
⅓ cup thickened cream
¼ cup chopped pepperoni
⅓ cup grated mozzarella cheese
2 teaspoons Italian seasoning
½ teaspoon baking powder
⅛ teaspoon salt
1 ½ tablespoons grated Parmesan cheese
½ cup no-added-sugar napolitana sauce, warmed

1. Preheat air fryer at 150°C for 3 minutes.
2. In a medium bowl, combine eggs with coconut flour, cassava flour, thickened cream, pepperoni, mozzarella cheese, Italian seasoning, baking powder and salt.
3. Pour batter into an ungreased pizza pan.
4. Place pan in air fryer basket and cook for 19 minutes. Sprinkle Parmesan cheese on top and cook for an additional minute.
5. Remove pan from basket and let set for 5 minutes, then slice and serve with warmed napolitana sauce.

PER SERVING

CALORIES: 226 | **FAT:** 17g | **PROTEIN:** 10g | **SODIUM:** 563mg | **FIBRE:** 2g | **CARBOHYDRATES:** 10g | **NET CARBOHYDRATES:** 7g | **SUGAR:** 3g

CASSAVA FLOUR

Cassava flour is derived from the cassava root — it is gluten free and a great replacement for wheat flour. While it is available at specialty stores and online, it may be difficult to find. Try substituting it with tapioca flour. Or, if gluten isn't a problem, simply substitute your cassava flour with plain flour.

Chipotle Avocado Fries

This will become your new addictive, fantastically awesome snack. The air fryer crisps up the outside evenly, and the avocado becomes almost creamy when heated. The soothing nature of the avocado pairs nicely with the heat from the chipotle, but if spice isn't your thing, swap the chipotle powder for some milder smoked paprika.

Hands-On Time: 10 minutes
Cook Time: 10 minutes

Serves 2

- **1 large egg, beaten**
- **¼ cup almond flour**
- **1 ½ tablespoons ground flaxseed**
- **¼ teaspoon chipotle powder**
- **¼ teaspoon salt**
- **1 large avocado, peeled, pitted and sliced into 8 "fries"**

1. Preheat air fryer to 190°C for 3 minutes.
2. Place egg in a small dish. Combine almond flour, flaxseed, chipotle powder and salt in a separate shallow dish.
3. Dip avocado slices into egg. Toss through flour mixture to coat. Place half of slices in air fryer basket lightly greased with olive oil.
4. Cook for 5 minutes. Transfer to a medium serving plate and repeat cooking with remaining avocado slices.
5. Serve warm.

PER SERVING

KILOJOULES: 1397 | **FAT:** 29g | **PROTEIN:** 10g | **SODIUM:** 351mg | **FIBRE:** 11g | **CARBOHYDRATES:** 15g | **NET CARBOHYDRATES:** 4g | **SUGAR:** 1g

DOES FLAXSEED NEED TO BE GROUND?

Whole flaxseed that has not been ground often ends up going through your digestive system in its whole form. This is fine; however, in this form your body does not reap the health benefits that can be achieved with ground flaxseed.

Mozzarella Sticklets

This is a mini version of those deep-fried delights found on many appetiser menus — minus the oil. Serve these mini sticks with toothpicks and a warm napolitana sauce.

Hands-On Time: 15 minutes
Cook Time: 10 minutes

Serves 6

1 1/2 tablespoons plain flour
1 large egg
1 tablespoon full-cream milk
1/2 cup plain bread crumbs
1/4 teaspoon salt
1/4 teaspoon Italian seasoning
280 grams mozzarella cheese block, cut into sticks
2 teaspoons olive oil

1. In a small bowl, add flour.
2. In another small bowl, whisk together egg and milk.
3. Combine bread crumbs, salt and Italian seasoning in a shallow dish.
4. Roll a mozzarella sticklet in flour, then dip in egg mixture and then roll in bread crumb mixture. Shake off excess between each step. Set aside on a plate and repeat with remaining mozzarella. Place in freezer for 10 minutes.
5. Preheat air fryer at 200°C for 3 minutes.
6. Place half of mozzarella sticklets in fryer basket. Cook for 2 minutes. Shake. Lightly brush with olive oil. Cook for an additional 2 minutes. Shake. Cook for an additional 1 minute. Transfer to a serving dish.
7. Repeat with remaining sticklets and serve warm.

PER SERVING

KILOJOULES: 824 | **FAT:** 12g | **PROTEIN:** 13g | **SODIUM:** 471mg | **FIBRE:** 0g | **CARBOHYDRATES:** 9g | **NET CARBOHYDRATES:** 9g | **SUGAR:** 1g

Five Spice Crunchy Edamame

Crispy on the outside and slightly tender on the inside, these snackable bites deliver a healthy dose of fibre, vitamins and minerals.

Hands-On Time: 5 minutes
Cook Time: 16 minutes

Serves 4

- **1 cup ready-to-eat edamame, shelled**
- **3/4 tablespoon sesame oil**
- **1 teaspoon five spice powder**
- **1/2 teaspoon salt**

1. Preheat air fryer at 180°C for 3 minutes.
2. In a small bowl, toss edamame in sesame oil. Place in air fryer basket and cook for 5 minutes. Shake. Cook for an additional 5 minutes. Shake. Cook for an additional 6 minutes.
3. Transfer to a small bowl and toss with five spice powder and salt. Let cool and serve.

PER SERVING

KILOJOULES: 259 | **FAT:** 5g | **PROTEIN:** 3g | **SODIUM:** 292mg | **FIBRE:** 1g | **CARBOHYDRATES:** 2g | **NET CARBOHYDRATES:** 1g | **SUGAR:** 1g

Spicy Sunflower Seeds

Sunflower seeds are a protein powerhouse filled with vitamins and minerals. Crisp them up with a little heat in your air fryer for a lovely treat.

Hands-On Time: 10 minutes
Cook Time: 10 minutes

Serves 4

- **2 cups unsalted sunflower seeds**
- **2 teaspoons olive oil**
- **2 teaspoons chilli garlic paste**
- **1/4 teaspoon salt**
- **1 teaspoon erythritol sweetener**

1. Preheat air fryer at 160°C for 3 minutes.
2. Combine all ingredients in a medium bowl until seeds are well coated.
3. Place seeds in ungreased air fryer basket. Cook for 5 minutes. Shake basket. Cook for an additional 5 minutes.
4. Transfer to a medium serving bowl and serve.

PER SERVING

KILOJOULES: 1661 | **FAT:** 34g | **PROTEIN:** 13g | **SODIUM:** 157mg | **FIBRE:** 7g | **CARBOHYDRATES:** 17g | **NET CARBOHYDRATES:** 9g | **SUGAR:** 2g

Roasted Pumpkin Seeds

The air fryer roasts pumpkin seeds for crunchy snacking, so you can enjoy low-carb, antioxidant-rich bites for a snack on the run. If you can't get all of the pumpkin guts off of the seeds once you've removed them, don't sweat it — they are edible and add a little extra flavour!

Hands-On Time: 10 minutes
Cook Time: 13 minutes

Serves 4

- **2 cups fresh pumpkin seeds**
- **3/4 tablespoon butter, melted**
- **1 teaspoon salt, divided**
- **1/2 teaspoon onion powder**
- **1/2 teaspoon dried parsley**
- **1/2 teaspoon garlic powder**
- **1/2 teaspoon dried dill**
- **1/4 teaspoon dried chives**
- **1/4 teaspoon dry mustard**
- **1/4 teaspoon celery seed**
- **1/4 teaspoon freshly ground black pepper**

1. Preheat air fryer at 160°C for 3 minutes.
2. In a medium bowl, toss seeds with butter and 1/2 teaspoon salt.
3. Place seed mixture in ungreased air fryer basket and cook for 7 minutes. Using a spatula, turn seeds, then cook for an additional 6 minutes.
4. Transfer to a medium serving bowl. Toss with remaining ingredients. Serve.

PER SERVING

KILOJOULES: 1627 | **FAT:** 29g | **PROTEIN:** 22g | **SODIUM:** 583mg | **FIBRE:** 4g | **CARBOHYDRATES:** 9g | **NET CARBOHYDRATES:** 4g | **SUGAR:** 0g

Greek Devilled Eggs

Devilled eggs hark back to the days when bell-bottoms and disco were all the rage. But has this delicious egg treat ever really gone out of fashion? Embrace fusion and try this new take on a classic.

Hands-On Time: 5 minutes
Cook Time: 15 minutes

Serves 4

- 4 large eggs
- 1 cup ice cubes
- 1 cup water
- 1 1/2 tablespoons plain Greek yoghurt
- 1 1/2 tablespoons pitted and finely chopped kalamata olives
- 1 1/2 tablespoons goat cheese crumbled
- 1/8 teaspoon salt
- 1/8 teaspoon freshly ground black pepper
- 1 1/2 tablespoons finely chopped fresh mint

1. Preheat air fryer at 120°C for 3 minutes.
2. Place eggs in silicone muffin cups to avoid bumping around and cracking during cooking process. Add silicone cups to air fryer basket. Cook for 15 minutes.
3. Add ice and water to a medium bowl. Transfer eggs to water bath immediately to stop cooking process. After 5 minutes, carefully peel eggs.
4. Cut eggs in half lengthwise. Spoon yolks into a separate medium bowl. Arrange white halves on a large plate.
5. Using a fork, blend egg yolks with yoghurt, olives, goat cheese, salt and pepper. Spoon mixture into white halves. Garnish with mint and serve.

PER SERVING

CALORIES: 109 | **FAT:** 8g | **PROTEIN:** 8g | **SODIUM:** 290mg | **FIBRE:** 0g | **CARBOHYDRATES:** 1g | **NET CARBOHYDRATES:** 1g | **SUGAR:** 1g

WHY CUT THE EGGS LENGTHWISE?

Not only can you turn the devilled egg ingredient list on its head, but you can also try cutting the egg at its width instead of lengthwise. The white part of the egg is more distributed with the yolk filling instead of having one great bite and then one bite with mostly egg whites. Cutting the egg in this different fashion yields a more balanced bite each time.

California Roll Devilled Eggs

If you love the flavours of sushi but rolling your own seems daunting, try this completely accessible take on a sushi roll classic!

Hands-On Time: 5 minutes
Cook Time: 15 minutes

Serves 4

- **4 large eggs**
- **1 cup ice cubes**
- **1 cup water**
- **1 1/2 tablespoons mayonnaise**
- **1/2 teaspoon coconut aminos**
- **1/4 medium ripe avocado, peeled, pitted and diced**
- **1/4 teaspoon wasabi powder**
- **1 1/2 tablespoons diced cucumber**
- **1/4 cup lump crabmeat, shells discarded**
- **1 sheet nori, sliced**
- **8 slices jarred pickled ginger**
- **1 teaspoon toasted sesame seeds**

1. Preheat air fryer at 120°C for 3 minutes.
2. Place eggs in silicone muffin cups to avoid bumping around and cracking during cooking process. Add silicone cups to air fryer basket. Cook for 15 minutes.
3. Add ice and water to a medium bowl. Transfer eggs to water bath immediately to stop cooking process. After 5 minutes, carefully peel eggs.
4. Cut eggs in half lengthwise. Spoon yolks into a medium bowl. Arrange white halves on a large plate.
5. Using a fork, blend egg yolks, mayonnaise, coconut aminos, avocado and wasabi powder until smooth. Mix in diced cucumber. Spoon into white halves.
6. Garnish eggs with crabmeat, nori and pickled ginger. Sprinkle with sesame seeds and serve.

PER SERVING

KILOJOULS: 684 | **FAT:** 12g | **PROTEIN:** 8g | **SODIUM:** 293mg | **FIBRE:** 2g | **CARBOHYDRATES:** 3g | **NET CARBOHYDRATES:** 1g | **SUGAR:** 0g

Barbecue Turnip Chips

Slicing the turnips paper-thin and consistently is the key to perfect turnip chips. The air fryer will brown the edges, but keep checking them toward the end of the cooking time, as they can go from brown to burned quickly!

Hands-On Time: 10 minutes
Cook Time: 24 minutes

Serves 2

1/2 teaspoon smoked paprika
1/4 teaspoon chilli powder
1/4 teaspoon garlic powder
1/8 teaspoon onion powder
1/8 teaspoon cayenne pepper
1/8 teaspoon erythritol sweetener
1 teaspoon salt, divided
1 large turnip, sliced into 3mm-thick circles
2 teaspoons olive oil

1. Preheat air fryer to 200°C for 3 minutes.
2. In a small bowl, combine paprika, chilli powder, garlic powder, onion powder, cayenne pepper, erythritol and 1/2 teaspoon salt. Set aside.
3. In a medium bowl, toss turnip slices with olive oil and 1/2 teaspoon salt.
4. Place half of turnip slices in air fryer basket lightly greased with olive oil and cook for 6 minutes. Shake basket and cook for an additional 6 minutes.
5. Transfer chips to a medium bowl and repeat cooking with remaining turnip slices. Toss with seasoning mix. Let rest for 15 minutes, then serve.

PER SERVING

KILOJOULES: 297 | **FAT:** 5g | **PROTEIN:** 1g | **SODIUM:** 1,235mg | **FIBRE:** 2g | **CARBOHYDRATES:** 7g | **NET CARBOHYDRATES:** 5g | **SUGAR:** 4g

Pimiento Cheese Jalapeño Poppers

This classic Southern spread of cheese, mayonnaise and pimientos is traditionally served in a sandwich or with crackers, but it makes the perfect filling for spicy jalapeño boats. Because the peppers are seeded, most of the heat is removed. If you like things spicy, though, mix the seeds in with the pimiento cheese to kick it up a notch!

Hands-On Time: 10 minutes
Cook Time: 8 minutes

Makes 10 poppers

- **½ cup pimiento cheese (see note)**
- **5 medium jalapeños, halved lengthwise and seeded**

HOW TO MAKE PIMIENTO CHEESE

This cheese spread is super versatile — you can dip it, spread it, mix it or stuff it like we have with these Jalapeño Poppers. Just combine 450 grams of finely shredded Cheddar cheese with 1 (110 gram) jar pimientos including juice, ½ cup mayonnaise, ¼ teaspoon salt and ¼ teaspoon freshly ground black pepper. Refrigerate covered until ready to use.

1. Preheat air fryer at 180°C for 3 minutes.
2. Press pimiento cheese into each jalapeño half.
3. Lay stuffed peppers in ungreased air fryer basket. Cook for 8 minutes.
4. Transfer to a large serving plate and serve warm.

PER SERVING (1 POPPER)

KILOJOULES: 159 | **FAT:** 3g | **PROTEIN:** 1g | **SODIUM:** 144mg | **FIBRE:** 0g | **CARBOHYDRATES:** 2g | **NET CARBOHYDRATES:** 2g | **SUGAR:** 0g

Chicken Enchilada Dip

Serve this ooey-gooey yumminess with your favourite carrot sticks, celery stalks or whatever produce your heart desires. The crudités just act as vessels to get this goodness to your mouth. Who needs tortilla chips?! Also, if you like coriander, garnish this dip with a little of this fresh herb (or parsley if you prefer) for a gorgeous presentation and added flavour!

Hands-On Time: 10 minutes
Cook Time: 10 minutes

Serves 6

- 230 grams cream cheese, room temperature
- 1/4 cup mayonnaise
- 1/4 cup sour cream
- 1 cup chopped cooked chicken breast
- 1 1/2 tablespoons peeled and chopped brown onion
- 110 grams canned diced green chillies, including juice
- 1 medium jalapeño chilli, seeded and minced
- 1 cup shredded Cheddar cheese, divided
- 1/4 cup cored, seeded and diced fresh vine-ripe tomatoes

1. Preheat air fryer to 200°C for 3 minutes.
2. In a large bowl, mix cream cheese, mayonnaise and sour cream until smooth. Add chicken, onion, green chillies, jalapeño and 1/2 cup Cheddar cheese.
3. Spoon mixture into an ungreased 15cm oven-safe baking dish. Sprinkle remaining cheese on top.
4. Place dish in air fryer basket. Cook for 10 minutes.
5. Garnish cooked dip with diced tomatoes and serve warm.

PER SERVING

KILOJOULS: 1393 | **FAT:** 29g | **PROTEIN:** 14g | **SODIUM:** 395mg | **FIBRE:** 1g | **CARBOHYDRATES:** 5g | **NET CARBOHYDRATES:** 4g | **SUGAR:** 2g

Jalapeño Popper Bites

These are so tasty! The flavours meld together, and the air fryer crisps these bites up to perfection. And you'll never even know the carb-filled potatoes are missing.

Hands-On Time: 10 minutes
Cook Time: 18 minutes

Serves 4

- ³⁄₄ cup riced cauliflower
- 2 medium jalapeños, seeded and minced
- 1 large egg
- ¹⁄₃ cup grated Cheddar cheese
- 28 grams cream cheese, room temperature
- ³⁄₄ tablespoon peeled and grated brown onion
- ¹⁄₃ cup almond flour
- ¹⁄₂ teaspoon salt
- ¹⁄₄ teaspoon garlic powder

1. Preheat air fryer at 190°C for 3 minutes.
2. In a medium bowl, combine all ingredients. Form into 12 rectangular mounds (about 1 tablespoon each).
3. Cut a piece of baking paper to fit bottom of air fryer basket. Place six pieces on baking paper in basket. Cook for 9 minutes. Transfer to a medium serving plate and repeat cooking with remaining pieces.
4. Let rest for 5 minutes, then serve warm.

PER SERVING

KILOJOULES: 598 | **FAT:** 12g | **PROTEIN:** 7g | **SODIUM:** 403mg | **FIBRE:** 2g | **CARBOHYDRATES:** 5g | **NET CARBOHYDRATES:** 3g | **SUGAR:** 1g

Cauliflower Pizza Crusts

There are so many options becoming available in the produce section of supermarkets these days. You can also find broccoli rice — and even a cauli-brocco mixture. Get creative and try these in the following recipe. You may finally be able to get those picky eaters to eat their vegetables! To make your pizza, top the crust with your favorite toppings and cook in the air fryer for 3 minutes at 200°C.

Hands-On Time: 10 minutes
Cook Time: 24 minutes

Serves 2

- **1 cup cauliflower rice**
- **1 large egg**
- **1/2 cup grated mozzarella cheese**
- **3/4 tablespoon grated Parmesan cheese**
- **1 clove garlic, peeled and minced**
- **1 teaspoon Italian seasoning**
- **1/8 teaspoon salt**

CAULIFLOWER RICE

Although pre-made cauliflower rice can be purchased in most produce or frozen food sections, cauliflower rice is actually very easy to make. The easiest way is to simply grate one head of cauliflower on a box grater. You can also place florets in a blender with 1 cup of water and blend until desired consistency. Then simply strain out the water and pat dry with paper towels.

1. Preheat air fryer at 200°F for 3 minutes.
2. In a medium bowl, combine all ingredients. Divide mixture in half and spread into two pizza pans greased with cooking spray.
3. Place one pizza pan in air fryer basket and cook for 12 minutes. Remove pan from basket and repeat cooking with second pan.

PER SERVING

KILOJOULES: 468 | **FAT:** 6g | **PROTEIN:** 10g | **SODIUM:** 357mg | **FIBRE:** 1g | **CARBOHYDRATES:** 4g | **NET CARBOHYDRATES:** 3g | **SUGAR:** 1g

Bone Marrow Butter

When bone marrow is cooked, it becomes rich and smooth like butter. So, imagine adding it to actual butter — it is a combination that is beyond delicious. Once your steak is off the grill, cut off a slice of this butter and let it melt atop the meat. Or, if you are cooking your beef on the stove, cook it in a little bone marrow butter. Either way, it is sinfully good!

Hands-On Time: 10 minutes
Cook Time: 12 minutes

Serves 4

910 grams beef bone marrow bones, cut into 5cm sections
2 cloves garlic, peeled and quartered
3 3/4 tablespoons butter, softened
3/4 tablespoon chopped fresh thyme leaves
1/4 teaspoon salt

1. Soak bones in water in a large bowl and refrigerate for 1 hour.
2. Preheat air fryer at 200°C for 3 minutes.
3. Place bones in ungreased air fryer basket. Cook for 12 minutes.
4. Remove from basket and let cool for 10 minutes, then push marrow out of bones with a small knife or chopstick. Add to a food processor with remaining ingredients and pulse until smooth.
5. Place mixture on a piece of plastic wrap. Fold sides in to create a log. Spin ends until log is tight. Refrigerate for 1 hour until firm.

PER SERVING

KILOJOULES: 895 | **FAT:** 23g | **PROTEIN:** 1g | **SODIUM:** 148mg | **FIBRE:** 0g | **CARBOHYDRATES:** 1g | **NET CARBOHYDRATES:** 1g | **SUGAR:** 0g

THE DIFFERENCE BETWEEN BONE MARROW BONES AND SOUP BONES

Both bones have marrow, but bone marrow bones are generally cut into 5cm sections with a visible view of the marrow tunnel, making it easier to cook and retrieve the marrow for butter. Soup bones tend to be longer, sometimes with more meat attached, and are more suited for beef bone broth.

Eggplant Parmie Sticks

A parmie (or parma depending on where you're from or your preference) is a classic ham and Parmesan cheese topping and a favourite across the country. We've created an easy low-carb version by adding it to eggplant and switching out the ham for crushed pork rinds. For extra nutritional value, keep the skins on your eggplant sticks.

Hands-On Time: 10 minutes
Cook Time: 24 minutes

Serves 4

- 2 large eggs
- 1 ½ tablespoons thickened cream
- ½ cup crushed pork rinds
- ½ cup grated Parmesan cheese
- ½ teaspoon salt
- 1 medium eggplant, cut into 1cm rounds, then sliced into sticks
- ½ cup no-sugar-added napolitana sauce, warmed

1. Preheat air fryer to 200°C for 3 minutes.
2. Whisk together eggs and heavy cream in a medium bowl. In a separate shallow dish, combine pork rinds, Parmesan cheese and salt.
3. Dip eggplant sticks in egg mixture. Coat in pork rind mixture. Place half of the eggplant sticks in air fryer basket lightly greased with olive oil.
4. Cook for 6 minutes, then flip and cook for an additional 6 minutes. Repeat with remaining eggplant sticks.
5. Transfer to a large serving plate and serve with warmed napolitana sauce for dipping.

PER SERVING

KILOJOULES: 695 | **FAT:** 10g | **PROTEIN:** 11g | **SODIUM:** 631mg | **FIBRE:** 4g | **CARBOHYDRATES:** 10g | **NET CARBOHYDRATES:** 6g | **SUGAR:** 6g

Low-Carb Honey Mustard

This sauce is an American classic and can be used in so many ways, especially with air-fried vegetables or as a dressing for salads.

Hands-On Time: 10 minutes
Cook Time: 0 minutes

Makes 3/4 cup

- **1/4 cup mayonnaise**
- **1 1/2 tablespoons yellow mustard**
- **1 teaspoon Dijon mustard**
- **1/4 teaspoon apple cider vinegar**
- **3/4 tablespoon erythritol sweetener**

Combine all ingredients in a small bowl. Refrigerate covered up to five days until ready to use.

PER SERVING (1 TEASPOON)

KILOJOULES: 50 | **FAT:** 1g | **PROTEIN:** 0g | **SODIUM:** 25mg | **FIBRE:** 0g | **CARBOHYDRATES:** 0g | **NET CARBOHYDRATES:** 0g | **SUGAR:** 0g

4

Side Dishes

Eating a low-carb diet can seem daunting and boring — sometimes all in the same breath. Often, you tend to concentrate on the protein and don't take the time to fill your plate and body with any healthy sides. All the while, the fresh produce you carefully chose at the store or farmers' market takes a back seat in the refrigerator, eventually getting slimy, until you inevitably toss it out. Not only is it a waste of healthy food, but it is also a big waste of money. Luckily, the air fryer is here to save the day (and your meal). With the air fryer, you can have roasted, seasonal vegetables in minutes while the main dish is being prepared!

In this chapter, you'll find a range of easy, delicious and surprisingly low-carb side dishes. With recipes from Prosciutto-Wrapped Asparagus and Roasted Radishes to Citrus Spring Onions and Broccoli Bites, you will be happy you took those few extra moments to pop a side dish in the fryer. Your body and taste buds will thank you, too!

Dilly Dinner Muffins

Sometimes when eating a low-carb diet, you just want a piece of bread. Try these dilly dinner muffins! The dill pairs nicely with the protein in a salmon fillet or grilled chicken, and the feeling of eating bread again will satisfy that craving — without sabotaging your diet.

Hands-On Time: 10 minutes
Cook Time: 12 minutes

Serves 4

1 cup almond flour
1 teaspoon dried dill
1/8 teaspoon salt
1/4 teaspoon onion powder
2 teaspoons baking powder
1 large egg
1/4 cup plain Greek yoghurt
1/4 cup grated Parmesan cheese

1. Preheat air fryer at 180°C for 3 minutes.
2. In a medium bowl, combine almond flour, dill, salt, onion powder and baking powder. Set aside.
3. In a separate small bowl, whisk together egg, yoghurt and Parmesan cheese. Add wet ingredients to dry ingredients and combine until blended.
4. Transfer batter to six silicone muffin cups lightly greased with olive oil. Place muffin cups in air fryer basket and cook for 12 minutes.
5. Serve warm.

PER SERVING

KILOJOULES: 904 | **FAT:** 17g | **PROTEIN:** 11g | **SODIUM:** 372mg | **FIBRE:** 3g | **CARBOHYDRATES:** 8g | **NET CARBOHYDRATES:** 5g | **SUGAR:** 2g

Hot Dog Bread

This bread is just fun. It gives you that pigs-in-a-blanket feel without any of the carb-laden guilt. And don't forget to buy some mustard or no-sugar-added tomato sauce, or make some ketchup at home, to dip this in for the full experience!

Hands-On Time: 5 minutes
Cook Time: 10 minutes

Serves 4

- **½ cup finely ground almond flour**
- **¼ cup arrowroot flour**
- **¾ tablespoon erythritol sweetener**
- **½ teaspoon baking powder**
- **¼ teaspoon salt**
- **1 ½ tablespoons butter, melted**
- **¾ tablespoon no-added-sugar tomato paste**
- **1 large egg**
- **½ teaspoon unflavoured gelatin**
- **1 teaspoon dried thyme**
- **2 beef hot dogs, cut into 1cm sections**

1. Preheat air fryer at 150°C for 3 minutes.
2. In a large bowl, combine flours, erythritol, baking powder and salt. Set aside.
3. In a small bowl, combine butter, tomato paste, egg, gelatin and thyme. Add butter mixture to flour mixture and stir until smooth. Fold in hot dogs.
4. Spoon mixture into an ungreased pizza pan. Place pan in air fryer basket and cook for 10 minutes.
5. Remove from basket and let set for 5 minutes, then slice and serve warm.

PER SERVING

KILOJOULES: 1079 | **FAT:** 21g | **PROTEIN:** 8g | **SODIUM:** 427mg | **FIBRE:** 2g | **CARBOHYDRATES:** 14g | **NET CARBOHYDRATES:** 9g | **SUGAR:** 1g

Roasted Radishes

Try this dish next to a juicy steak to take the place of a traditional potato side. The garlic and butter transform the meaty-textured radish into a fantastic recipe — without the guilt of a high carb count.

Hands-On Time: 10 minutes
Cook Time: 10 minutes

Serves 2

1 1/2 tablespoons butter, melted
2 cloves garlic, peeled and minced
1/4 teaspoon salt
20 medium radishes, ends trimmed, quartered
1 1/2 tablespoons goat cheese crumbles
3/4 tablespoon chopped fresh parsley

1. Preheat air fryer at 190°C for 3 minutes.
2. In a medium bowl, combine butter, garlic and salt. Toss radishes in mixture.
3. Place radishes in ungreased air fryer basket. Cook for 5 minutes. Shake basket, then cook for an additional 5 minutes.
4. Transfer to a large serving dish. Toss with goat cheese and garnish with parsley. Serve warm.

PER SERVING

KILOJOULES: 640 | **FAT:** 14g | **PROTEIN:** 3g | **SODIUM:** 367mg | **FIBRE:** 2g | **CARBOHYDRATES:** 4g | **NET CARBOHYDRATES:** 3g | **SUGAR:** 2g

Prosciutto-Wrapped Asparagus

The air fryer knows how to crisp up prosciutto and there's no need for seasoning. The salty nature of prosciutto lends just enough flavour for these tasty spears.

Hands-On Time: 10 minutes
Cook Time: 12 minutes

Serves 4

85 grams prosciutto, sliced lengthwise into 18 slices
18 thick asparagus spears, trimmed of woody ends

1. Spiral wrap the prosciutto strips from the bottom of the asparagus to the top, stopping before covering the tip.
2. Preheat air fryer at 200°C for 3 minutes.
3. Place wrapped asparagus in ungreased air fryer basket. Cook for 6 minutes. Shake. Cook for an additional 6 minutes until prosciutto is crisp.
4. Transfer to a plate and serve.

PER SERVING

KILOJOULES: 234 | **FAT:** 2g | **PROTEIN:** 7g | **SODIUM:** 574mg | **FIBRE:** 1g | **CARBOHYDRATES:** 3g | **NET CARBOHYDRATES:** 1g | **SUGAR:** 1g

Baked Fennel

Fennel's distinct anise, or liquorice, flavour tends to tame once heated. Add a squeeze of lemon and this side dish is perfect alongside proteins like chicken.

Hands-On Time: 5 minutes
Cook Time: 8 minutes

Serves 2

1 large fennel bulb, fronds removed and reserved, sliced
2 teaspoons olive oil
1/4 teaspoon salt
2 lemon wedges
3/4 tablespoon chopped fennel fronds

1. Preheat air fryer at 180°C for 3 minutes.
2. Brush fennel slices on both sides with olive oil and season with salt.
3. Place fennel slices in ungreased air fryer basket. Cook for 8 minutes.
4. Transfer to a medium serving dish. Squeeze lemon on fennel and garnish with chopped fronds. Serve warm.

PER SERVING

KILOJOULES: 326 | **FAT:** 5g | **PROTEIN:** 2g | **SODIUM:** 353mg | **FIBRE:** 4g | **CARBOHYDRATES:** 9g | **NET CARBOHYDRATES:** 5g | **SUGAR:** 5g

Roasted Red Capsicum

You'll find pre-made roasted red capsicum in store, but why spend that money when they are so easy to make with your air fryer for a fraction of the price? They can be added in salads, placed on pizzas, chopped up in devilled eggs, folded into frittatas and used wherever else your imagination takes you.

Hands-On Time: 10 minutes
Cook Time: 24 minutes

Serves 2

2 large red capsicums, tops and bottoms removed, cut along rib sections and seeded
1 1/2 tablespoons olive oil

THE MANY COLOURS OF CAPSICUM

In addition to red capsicum, there are also green, yellow, orange and even white and purple. Follow the Roasted Red Capsicum recipe using your capsicum colour of choice. Even switch it up from recipe to recipe. Each colour yields different nutrient components, so check labels or look up nutritional information online. Variety is the spice of life — give the variety of colours a chance and enhance your health benefits!

1. Preheat air fryer at 200°C for 3 minutes.
2. In a small bowl, toss pepper sections with olive oil.
3. Arrange sections in ungreased air fryer basket. Cook for 12 minutes. Flip capsicums and cook for an additional 12 minutes.
4. Transfer capsicums to a small metal bowl. Cover bowl with plastic wrap and let rest for 15 minutes to allow further steaming to occur.
5. Remove capsicums from bowl. Peel and discard skins from capsicums. Serve.

PER SERVING

KILOJOULES: 711 | **FAT:** 14g | **PROTEIN:** 2g | **SODIUM:** 7mg | **FIBRE:** 3g | **CARBOHYDRATES:** 10g | **NET CARBOHYDRATES:** 7g | **SUGAR:** 7g

Spaghetti Squash with Avocado Carbonara

Spaghetti alla carbonara is a fantastically rich southern Italian meal. It almost tastes like an alfredo; however, there is no cream used. The creaminess comes from the eggs and the Parmesan cheese. In this dish, there is avocado added for healthy fat and the carb-filled pasta is replaced with spaghetti squash.

Hands-On Time: 5 minutes
Cook Time: 32 minutes

Serves 4

- 2 teaspoons olive oil
- 1 (700 gram) spaghetti squash, halved and seeded
- 1 medium ripe avocado, peeled and pitted
- 1/4 cup chicken broth
- 1 large egg
- 1 1/2 tablespoons grated Parmesan cheese
- 1/4 teaspoon salt
- 2 slices sugar-free bacon
- 1/4 cup chopped fresh parsley

1. Preheat air fryer at 190°C for 3 minutes.
2. Rub olive oil over both halves of spaghetti squash. Place flat sides down in ungreased air fryer basket. Cook for 25 minutes.
3. While squash is cooking, blend together avocado, chicken broth, egg, Parmesan cheese and salt in a medium bowl. Set aside.
4. In a large frying pan, cook bacon over medium heat for 5 minutes until crispy. Transfer cooked bacon to a paper towel to cool for 5 minutes, then crumble.
5. Transfer cooked squash to a cutting board and let cool for 5 minutes until easy to handle. Using a fork, gently pull strands out of squash. Transfer strands to same frying pan.
6. Add avocado mixture and parsley to frying pan. Over medium heat, toss spaghetti squash with sauce for 2 minutes until well coated. Add bacon crumbles.
7. Transfer to a large serving dish and serve warm.

PER SERVING

KILOJOULES: 774 | **FAT:** 13g | **PROTEIN:** 6g | **SODIUM:** 364mg | **FIBRE:** 6g | **CARBOHYDRATES:** 14g | **NET CARBOHYDRATES:** 9g | **SUGAR:** 4g

Parmesan Thyme Cauliflower

This recipe yields a nice cauliflower side dish that can be served with any protein of your choice. If you prefer your cauliflower a little more tender, just add a few minutes to your cooking time.

Hands-On Time: 10 minutes
Cook Time: 12 minutes

Serves 4

- **1 1/4 tablespoons butter, melted**
- **1 1/2 tablespoons grated Parmesan cheese**
- **2 teaspoons dried thyme**
- **1/2 teaspoon garlic powder**
- **1/4 teaspoon salt**
- **1 large head cauliflower, chopped into small florets**

1. Preheat air fryer at 180°C for 3 minutes.
2. In a large bowl, combine butter, Parmesan cheese, thyme, garlic powder and salt. Toss in florets.
3. Place half of cauliflower mixture in ungreased air fryer basket. Cook for 3 minutes. Shake basket, then cook for an additional 3 minutes.
4. Transfer cooked cauliflower to a large serving bowl. Repeat cooking with remaining cauliflower. Serve warm.

PER SERVING

KILOJOULES: 594 | **FAT:** 10g | **PROTEIN:** 5g | **SODIUM:** 252mg | **FIBRE:** 4g | **CARBOHYDRATES:** 11g | **NET CARBOHYDRATES:** 7g | **SUGAR:** 4g

Creamy Cauli-Root Vegetable Mash

Although mashed potatoes are a staple dinner side, there are many vegetables that can replicate that creamy mouthful without the carbs. If you want to load this mash up, add some cooked bacon crumbles and grated Cheddar cheese and cook for another minute or two!

Hands-On Time: 10 minutes
Cook Time: 15 minutes

Serves 4

- 1 small head cauliflower, chopped into small florets
- 1 medium swede, peeled and small-diced
- 3 tablespoons butter, divided
- 1 teaspoon salt, divided
- 3 cloves garlic, peeled
- ½ teaspoon freshly ground black pepper
- 56 grams cream cheese, room temperature
- ½ cup unsweetened almond milk

1. Preheat air fryer at 180°C for 3 minutes.
2. In a large bowl, toss cauliflower florets and swede with 1 ½ tablespoons melted butter and ½ teaspoon salt.
3. Place mixture in ungreased air fryer basket. Cook for 5 minutes. Toss mixture, then cook for an additional 5 minutes. Add garlic. Cook for another 5 minutes.
4. Using a stand blender or food processor, blend or pulse cooked ingredients with remaining butter, remaining salt, pepper, cream cheese and almond milk.
5. Transfer to a large serving dish and serve warm.

PER SERVING

KILOJOULES: 899 | **FAT:** 17g | **PROTEIN:** 5g | **SODIUM:** 701mg | **FIBRE:** 4g | **CARBOHYDRATES:** 13g | **NET CARBOHYDRATES:** 9g | **SUGAR:** 6g

Seasoned Green Beans

You know the scenario: you've gone to the store or farmers' market and bought a bag of beautiful fresh green beans… but now what? They sit in the refrigerator for a long time and get a little rotten, maybe never making their way to your dinner plate at all. The air fryer is a quick way to cook those green beans, so you can enjoy them in almost any meal.

Hands-On Time: 5 minutes
Cook Time: 10 minutes

Serves 4

- 2 cups fresh green beans, ends trimmed
- 3/4 tablespoon butter, melted
- 1/2 teaspoon salt
- 1/4 teaspoon freshly ground black pepper
- 1 sugar-free bacon, diced
- 1 clove garlic, peeled and minced
- 1 lemon wedge

1. Preheat air fryer at 190°C for 3 minutes.
2. In a medium bowl, toss together green beans, butter, salt and pepper.
3. Add green beans to ungreased air fryer basket and cook for 5 minutes. Toss in bacon and cook for an additional 4 minutes. Toss in minced garlic and cook for an additional minute.
4. Transfer to a medium serving dish, squeeze lemon over beans and toss. Serve warm.

PER SERVING

KILOJOULES: 213 | **FAT:** 4g | **PROTEIN:** 2g | **SODIUM:** 331mg | **FIBRE:** 1g | **CARBOHYDRATES:** 4g | **NET CARBOHYDRATES:** 3g | **SUGAR:** 2g

Fried Artichoke Hearts

Because the artichoke hearts have already been softened and seasoned with salt and citrus from the lemon, it doesn't take much to flavour these fried vegetables. Serve as a side or atop a salad for a delicious change of pace.

Hands-On Time: 10 minutes
Cook Time: 14 minutes

Serves 4

1 large egg
3/4 tablespoon Dijon mustard
1/2 cup crushed pork rinds
1/4 cup almond flour
420 grams artichoke hearts in water, drained

1. Preheat air fryer at 180°C for 3 minutes.
2. In a medium bowl, whisk together egg and Dijon mustard.
3. In a separate shallow dish, combine pork rinds and almond flour.
4. Dip artichoke hearts in egg mixture, then coat in pork rind mixture.
5. Place half of prepared artichoke hearts in ungreased air fryer basket. Cook for 7 minutes.
6. Transfer to a large serving plate and repeat cooking with remaining artichokes. Serve warm.

PER SERVING

KILOJOULES: 448 | **FAT:** 6g | **PROTEIN:** 7g | **SODIUM:** 342mg | **FIBRE:** 1g | **CARBOHYDRATES:** 6g | **NET CARBOHYDRATES:** 2g | **SUGAR:** 0g

Bacony Mushrooms and Onions

Make this quick side dish to serve over a steak or next to a grilled chicken breast.

Hands-On Time: 10 minutes
Cook Time: 9 minutes

Serves 4

- 450 grams white button mushrooms, stems trimmed, halved
- 1 small brown onion, peeled and sliced into half-moons
- 4 slices sugar-free bacon, diced
- 1 clove garlic, peeled and minced

1. Preheat air fryer at 180°C for 3 minutes.
2. Place mushrooms, onion and bacon in ungreased air fryer basket. Cook for 5 minutes. Toss, then cook for another 3 minutes.
3. Add garlic to basket and cook for an additional minute.
4. Transfer to a medium serving dish and serve warm.

PER SERVING

KILOJOULES: 264 | **FAT:** 3g | **PROTEIN:** 6g | **SODIUM:** 151mg | **FIBRE:** 1g | **CARBOHYDRATES:** 6g | **NET CARBOHYDRATES:** 4g | **SUGAR:** 3g

Seasoned Roasted Asparagus

Because asparagus comes in many thicknesses, watch your cook time when making this dish. As far as colour, try the green, white or even purple asparagus for this recipe.

Hands-On Time: 5 minutes
Cook Time: 9 minutes

Serves 6

- 450 grams (about 30) medium-thick asparagus spears, woody ends discarded
- 3/4 tablespoon butter, melted
- 1/4 teaspoon salt
- 1 clove garlic, peeled and minced
- 2 teaspoons chopped fresh dill

1. Preheat air fryer at 190°C for 3 minutes.
2. In a large bowl, toss asparagus with butter.
3. Add asparagus to ungreased air fryer basket and cook for 5 minutes. Toss, then cook for an additional 4 minutes.
4. Transfer asparagus to a large serving dish and toss with salt, garlic and dill until coated. Serve warm.

PER SERVING

KILOJOULESS: 109 | **FAT:** 2g | **PROTEIN:** 1g | **SODIUM:** 98mg | **FIBRE:** 1g | **CARBOHYDRATES:** 2g | **NET CARBOHYDRATES:** 1g | **SUGAR:** 1g

Citrus Spring Onions

Often overlooked, this member of the *Allium* genus is more commonly used in Asian dishes. These small onions are quick and easy to cook, as well as much milder than a typical onion.

Hands-On Time: 5 minutes
Cook Time: 7 minutes

Serves 6

2 bunches fresh spring onions, ends trimmed to fit air fryer basket, halved lengthwise
3/4 tablespoon olive oil
2 teaspoons lime juice
1/4 teaspoon salt
1/4 teaspoon freshly ground black pepper
2 teaspoons lime zest

1. Preheat air fryer at 190°C for 3 minutes.
2. Toss spring onions with olive oil and lime juice in a large bowl.
3. Add spring onions to ungreased air fryer basket and cook for 4 minutes. Toss, then cook for an additional 3 minutes.
4. Transfer spring onions to a large serving dish and toss with salt and pepper. Garnish with lime zest. Serve warm.

PER SERVING

KILOJOULES: 125 | **FAT:** 2g | **PROTEIN:** 1g | **SODIUM:** 102mg | **FIBRE:** 1g | **CARBOHYDRATES:** 2g | **NET CARBOHYDRATES:** 2g | **SUGAR:** 1g

WHAT ABOUT THE CHOPPED-OFF SPRING ONIONS?

Some of the top greens are going to be cut off for uniformity and to fit in your air fryer basket. But there is no need to throw these away — place them in a container with water for up to one week, changing out the water every three days. These are a perfect flavour addition when making a bone broth or soup base.

Parsnips with Tahini Dressing

Parsnips are those carrot-looking white things that you may have passed by in the supermarket for years. They belong to the same family as carrots, but unlike with edible carrot greens, do not eat parsnip greens.

Hands-On Time: 10 minutes
Cook Time: 10 minutes

Serves 4

For Parsnips

- 1 teaspoon olive oil
- ½ teaspoon salt
- 3 large parsnips, peeled, halved lengthwise and cut into 3cm half-moons

For Tahini Dressing

- 1 tablespoon tahini
- 1 tablespoon fresh lemon juice
- 1 teaspoon water
- 1 clove garlic, peeled and minced
- 1 tablespoon chopped fresh parsley

1. **To make Parsnips:** Preheat air fryer at 190°C for 3 minutes.
2. In a medium bowl, whisk together olive oil and salt. Add parsnips and toss.
3. Add parsnips to ungreased air fryer basket and cook for 5 minutes. Toss, then cook for an additional 5 minutes.
4. **To make Tahini Dressing:** While parsnips are cooking, whisk together tahini, lemon juice, water and garlic in a medium bowl.
5. Add cooked parsnips and toss. Transfer to a medium serving dish. Garnish with parsley. Serve.

PER SERVING

KILJOULES: 343 | **FAT:** 3g | **PROTEIN:** 2g | **SODIUM:** 299mg | **FIBRE:** 3g | **CARBOHYDRATES:** 13g | **NET CARBOHYDRATES:** 9g | **SUGAR:** 3g

Simple Roasted Garlic

It is amazing how, after roasting garlic bulbs, you can squeeze the garlic out of the peel like butter. Great mixed in with "fauxtato" mashes, dips and even marinades, roasted garlic is magic — turning whatever it touches into gold!

Hands-On Time: 10 minutes
Cook Time: 45 minutes

Serves 8

1/4 cup avocado oil
2 bulbs garlic, unpeeled, 6mm removed from top
1/8 teaspoon salt

1. Preheat air fryer at 180°C for 3 minutes.
2. Drizzle avocado oil over garlic bulbs and rub it in with your finger. Season each bulb with salt.
3. Roll each bulb up in a square of aluminium foil. Place wrapped bulbs in ungreased air fryer basket. Cook for 45 minutes.
4. Unwrap each bulb. When cooled, squeeze roasted garlic from each clove and use as desired. Refrigerate unused bulbs in an air-tight container up to three days.

PER SERVING

KILOJOULESS: 130 | **FAT:** 0g | **PROTEIN:** 1g | **SODIUM:** 2mg | **FIBRE:** 0g | **CARBOHYDRATES:** 6g | **NET CARBOHYDRATES:** 6g | **SUGAR:** 0g

Chilli Lime Avocado Halves

Perfect on a low-carb diet, avocado lends such a healthy dose of fat and nutrients to your meals. And in addition to being filling, the avocado becomes creamier when heated.

Hands-On Time: 5 minutes
Cook Time: 7 minutes

Serves 4

- **2 teaspoons olive oil**
- **Juice of ½ medium lime**
- **2 medium avocados, halved, pitted and left in skins**
- **1 teaspoon chilli powder**
- **¼ teaspoon salt**

1. Preheat air fryer at 200°C for 3 minutes.
2. Combine olive oil and lime juice in a small bowl and brush over avocado halves.
3. Combine chilli powder and salt in a separate small bowl. Sprinkle over avocado halves.
4. Place avocado halves, cut sides up, in ungreased air fryer basket. Cook for 7 minutes.
5. Transfer to a serving plate and serve warm.

PER SERVING

KILOJOULESS: 770 | **FAT:** 17g | **PROTEIN:** 2g | **SODIUM:** 172mg | **FIBRE:** 7g | **CARBOHYDRATES:** 9g | **NET CARBOHYDRATES:** 2g | **SUGAR:** 1g

Zucchini Ribbons

Just like pasta, zucchini ribbons can be a side dish or a main meal depending on how you treat them or what you put on top of them.

Hands-On Time: 10 minutes
Cook Time: 3 minutes

Serves 4

- **2 medium zucchini (seed core discarded), peeled into thin ribbons**
- **2 teaspoons butter, melted**
- **¼ teaspoon salt**
- **¼ teaspoon freshly ground black pepper**

1. Preheat air fryer at 140°C for 3 minutes.
2. In a medium bowl, toss zucchini ribbons with butter, salt and pepper.
3. Place zucchini in ungreased air fryer basket and cook for 1 minute. Toss and cook for an additional 2 minutes.
4. Serve warm.

PER SERVING

KILOJOULES: 142 | **FAT:** 2g | **PROTEIN:** 1g | **SODIUM:** 153mg | **FIBRE:** 1g | **CARBOHYDRATES:** 3g | **NET CARBOHYDRATES:** 2g | **SUGAR:** 2g

Boursin-Stuffed Mushrooms

Boursin cheese has the consistency of cream cheese and is a product of Normandy. The magic of Boursin (and difference from cream cheese) is that it has already been seasoned for you. Boursin can be found with the specialty cheeses in the deli section of most supermarkets. It comes in a variety of flavours and can be used as a spread or in recipes such as this.

Hands-On Time: 10 minutes
Cook Time: 5 minutes

Serves 2

- 1 teaspoon olive oil
- 12 whole white button mushroom tops
- 1 1/2 tablespoons diced white button mushroom stems
- 3/4 tablespoon peeled and grated yellow onion
- 1/4 cup herbed Boursin cheese
- 1 1/2 tablespoons crushed pork rinds

1. Brush olive oil around top ridge of each mushroom top.
2. Preheat air fryer at 180°C for 3 minutes.
3. In a small bowl, combine mushroom stems, onion and Boursin cheese. Distribute and press mixture into tops of mushrooms. Sprinkle pork rinds on top.
4. Place stuffed mushrooms in ungreased air fryer basket. Cook for 5 minutes. Serve warm.

PER SERVING

KILOJOULESS: 745 | **FAT:** 15g | **PROTEIN:** 7g | **SODIUM:** 202mg | **FIBRE:** 1g | **CARBOHYDRATES:** 5g | **NET CARBOHYDRATES:** 4g | **SUGAR:** 3g

Baked Avocado with Burrata and Blistered Tomatoes

This dish is creamy times two: avocado and Burrata cheese are two velvety powerhouses which, when served with fresh tomatoes and basil, will blow your mind.

Hands-On Time: 5 minutes
Cook Time: 7 minutes

Serves 4

- **8 medium cherry tomatoes**
- **2 teaspoons olive oil**
- **2 medium avocados, halved, pitted and left in skins**
- **¼ teaspoon salt**
- **110 grams Burrata cheese**
- **2 tablespoons julienned fresh basil**

WHAT IS BURRATA?

Burrata is like the molten lava cake of cheeses. Encased in beautiful fresh mozzarella, the interior has a creamy, buttery consistency. Made from buffalo or cow's milk, Burrata is becoming increasingly mainstream in Australia and can be found with the specialty cheeses in the deli section of most supermarkets. It is generally sold in a plastic container of milky liquid.

1. Preheat air fryer at 190°C for 3 minutes.
2. Toss tomatoes in olive oil in a small bowl.
3. Place avocado halves, cut sides up, in ungreased air fryer basket. Scatter tomatoes around avocado halves. Cook for 7 minutes.
4. Place avocado halves on four small plates. Add two tomatoes to each half. Sprinkle salt over tomatoes. Tear Burrata cheese and evenly distribute over tomatoes. Garnish with basil. Serve.

PER SERVING

KILOJOULES: 1125 | **FAT:** 24g | **PROTEIN:** 7g | **SODIUM:** 240mg | **FIBRE:** 7g | **CARBOHYDRATES:** 10g | **NET CARBOHYDRATES:** 3g | **SUGAR:** 2g

Broccoli Bites

Broccoli is low in kilojoules and a good alternative to carb loaded veggies when you're following a low-carb diet. Give these bites of goodness a try — your family will fall in love!

Hands-On Time: 10 minutes
Cook Time: 18 minutes

Serves 4

- 1 cup riced broccoli
- 1 large egg
- 1/3 cup grated Cheddar cheese
- 28 grams cream cheese, room temperature
- 3/4 tablespoon peeled and grated brown onion
- 1/3 cup crushed pork rinds
- 1/2 teaspoon salt
- 1/4 teaspoon garlic powder

1. Preheat air fryer at 190°C for 3 minutes.
2. In a medium bowl, combine all ingredients. Form into 12 rectangular mounds (about 1 tablespoon each).
3. Cut a piece of baking paper to fit bottom of air fryer basket. Place six pieces on baking paper. Cook for 9 minutes. Transfer to a medium serving plate and repeat cooking with remaining pieces.
4. Let rest for 5 minutes, then serve warm.

PER SERVING

KILOJOULESS: 426 | **FAT:** 8g | **PROTEIN:** 7g | **SODIUM:** 449mg | **FIBRE:** 1g | **CARBOHYDRATES:** 2g | **NET CARBOHYDRATES:** 1g | **SUGAR:** 1g

WHERE DO I FIND BROCCOLI RICE?

Although pre-made broccoli rice can be purchased in most fresh produce or frozen food sections, broccoli rice is actually very easy to make. The easiest way is to simply grate a head of broccoli on a box grater or pulse in a food processor to desired consistency.

Crispy Zucchini Fries

These breaded crispy zucchini fries are excellent on their own, but they're even better dipped in a creamy rémoulade. A healthy alternative to drive-through French fries, this treat is delicious!

Hands-On Time: 10 minutes
Cook Time: 20 minutes

Serves 2

- **1 large zucchini, cut into 6mm fries**
- **1 teaspoon salt**
- **1 large egg**
- **3/4 tablespoon sour cream**
- **1/2 cup almond flour**
- **1/2 cup grated Parmesan cheese**

TRY THIS RÉMOULADE FOR DIPPING!

To whip up your own delicious rémoulade, simply combine the following ingredients and refrigerate covered up to three days until ready to use: 1/2 cup mayonnaise, 3/4 tablespoon Dijon mustard, 1 teaspoon smoked paprika, 1 teaspoon Cajun seasoning, 1 teaspoon prepared horseradish, 1/2 teaspoon dill pickle juice, 1/2 teaspoon Tabasco original hot sauce and 2 cloves peeled and minced garlic.

1. Scatter zucchini fries evenly over a paper towel. Sprinkle with salt. Let set for 10 minutes to pull out moisture, then pat with paper towels.
2. Preheat air fryer to 190°C for 3 minutes.
3. Whisk egg and sour cream together in a small bowl.
4. Combine almond flour and Parmesan cheese in a separate shallow dish.
5. Dip zucchini in egg mixture. Coat in flour mixture. Place half of zucchini in air fryer basket lightly greased with olive oil and cook for 5 minutes. Flip fries, then cook for an additional 5 minutes.
6. Transfer fries to a medium serving dish. Repeat with remaining zucchini fries and serve warm.

PER SERVING

KILOJOULES: 1330 | **FAT:** 24g | **PROTEIN:** 19g | **SODIUM:** 399mg | **FIBRE:** 4g | **CARBOHYDRATES:** 12g | **NET CARBOHYDRATES:** 5g | **SUGAR:** 5g

Turnip Fries with Bagel Seasoning

Have you ever wondered what to do with that weird little purplish-white orb in the produce section? Throw that turnip in your basket and give it a try with this tasty recipe. This root vegetable is loaded with fibre and nutrients and low in carbs!

Hands-On Time: 5 minutes
Cook Time: 15 minutes

Serves 4

- **2 medium turnips, peeled and cut into 6mm fries**
- **2 teaspoons avocado oil**
- **2 teaspoons bagel seasoning (see recipe below)**

1. Preheat air fryer to 200°C for 3 minutes.
2. In a medium bowl, toss fries with avocado oil and 1 teaspoon seasoning.
3. Place fries in air fryer basket lightly greased with olive oil and cook for 5 minutes. Shake basket and cook for an additional 5 minutes. Shake, then cook for another 5 minutes.
4. Transfer to a medium serving plate, garnish with remaining seasoning, and serve warm.

PER SERVING

KILOJOULES: 175 | **FAT:** 3g | **PROTEIN:** 1g | **SODIUM:** 235mg | **FIBRE:** 1g | **CARBOHYDRATES:** 4g | **NET CARBOHYDRATES:** 3g | **SUGAR:** 2g

BAGEL SEASONING

Bagel seasoning is a yummy mix of toppings you'd find on a bagel and tastes great on roasted vegetables or sprinkled on smashed avocado. Simply combine the following ingredients: 2 tablespoons toasted white sesame seeds, 1 ½ tablespoons toasted black sesame seeds, 1 ½ tablespoons dried onion flakes, 1 tablespoon dried garlic flakes, 1 tablespoon poppy seeds and 1 tablespoon salt flakes. Store in an airtight jar.

5

Chicken Main Dishes

Living a low-carb life can be lonely sometimes when your options feel limited. While chicken is affordable and packed with protein, you might assume you are confined to bland, limp breasts and drumsticks to avoid the carbs. But that's simply not the case! If you miss fried chicken, the air fryer is your new best friend. You are using a significantly lower amount of oil in the preparation, but the heat still gives it that crispiness on all sides. And because of the quicker cooking time, more nutrients stay intact and the chicken will be juicy and delicious.

Whether you're craving Cheesy Chicken Patties or your family is calling for Yoghurt Curry Chicken Legs, this chapter has a chicken recipe for every occasion. From Spicy Yellow Mustard Wings to Barbecue Chicken Meatballs, your new favourites are calling — so get frying!

Prep Day Chicken Breasts

This recipe is prepared simply so you can add the chicken breasts to a variety of other recipes. Cook them at the beginning of the week so they will be ready to add to a frittata, stir-fry, salad or soup during the week — or just heat them up and enjoy a simple meal.

Hands-On Time: 5 minutes
Cook Time: 9 minutes

Serves 4

- 2 teaspoons olive oil
- 2 (230 gram) boneless, skinless chicken breasts
- ½ teaspoon salt
- ¼ teaspoon freshly ground black pepper

1. Preheat air fryer at 180°C for 3 minutes.
2. Brush olive oil lightly over tops and bottom of chicken. Season with salt and pepper.
3. Add chicken to ungreased air fryer basket and cook for 4 minutes. Shake basket gently and flip chicken. Cook for an additional 5 minutes. Using a meat thermometer, ensure internal temperature is at least 75°C.
4. Transfer chicken to a large serving plate and let rest for 5 minutes, then chop into 3cm cubes and store covered and refrigerated up to one week.

PER SERVING

KILOJOULES: 652 | **FAT:** 5g | **PROTEIN:** 26g | **SODIUM:** 342mg | **FIBRE:** 0g | **CARBOHYDRATES:** 0g | **NET CARBOHYDRATES:** 0g | **SUGAR:** 0g

Pecan-Crusted Honey Mustard Chicken Breasts

Pulse your pecans into a meal instead of a flour — the chunkier texture will give a thicker coat. If you prefer a thinner coat, just pulse your pecans down a bit more. If you want to skip this step altogether, just purchase almond meal and proceed!

Hands-On Time: 5 minutes
Cook Time: 25 minutes

Serves 4

2 (170 gram) boneless, skinless chicken breasts, halved lengthwise
1/4 cup Low-Carb Honey Mustard (see recipe on page 62)
1/4 cup finely chopped pecans

1. Preheat air fryer at 180°C for 3 minutes.
2. Coat chicken with honey mustard.
3. Place pecans in a shallow dish. Coat chicken in pecans.
4. Add chicken to air fryer basket lightly greased with olive oil and cook for 10 minutes. Gently flip chicken and cook for an additional 15 minutes. Using a meat thermometer, ensure internal temperature is at least 75°C.
5. Transfer chicken to a large serving plate and let rest for 5 minutes before serving.

PER SERVING

KILOJOULES: 849 | **FAT:** 13g | **PROTEIN:** 20g | **SODIUM:** 147mg | **FIBRE:** 1g | **CARBOHYDRATES:** 3g | **NET CARBOHYDRATES:** 0g | **SUGAR:** 0g

Chicken Bulgogi with Riced Cauliflower and Pickled Cucumbers

Traditionally, bulgogi is a Korean barbecue beef dish; however, the dark meat of the chicken thigh is also a great venue for this delicious sauce. Coupled with the tameness of the cauliflower and the tanginess from the quick-pickled cucumbers, this is a complete one-bowl meal!

Hands-On Time: 15 minutes
Cook Time: 11 minutes

Serves 4

For Pickled Cucumbers

- 1 large continental cucumber, thinly sliced
- ¼ cup apple cider vinegar
- 2 cloves garlic, peeled and minced
- ½ teaspoon ground ginger
- ⅛ teaspoon chilli flakes
- 2 teaspoons erythritol sweetener
- ⅛ teaspoon salt

For Chicken Bulgogi

- 1 ½ tablespoons coconut aminos
- 2 teaspoons sesame oil
- 2 teaspoons erythritol sweetener
- ¾ tablespoon apple cider vinegar
- ¾ tablespoon fresh lime juice
- 2 cloves garlic, peeled and minced
- 2 teaspoons peeled and minced fresh ginger
- 3 spring onions, sliced, whites and greens separated, divided
- 680 grams (approximately 6) boneless, skinless chicken thighs, cut into 3cm cubes

Additional Ingredients

- 4 cups steamed cauliflower rice
- 2 teaspoons roasted sesame seeds

1. **To make Pickled Cucumbers:** Combine all ingredients in a medium bowl. Cover and refrigerate until ready to serve.
2. **To make Chicken Bulgogi:** In a large bowl, whisk together coconut aminos, sesame oil, erythritol, apple cider vinegar, lime juice, garlic, ginger and whites of spring onions. Add chicken and marinate for 10 minutes in refrigerator.
3. Preheat air fryer at 180°C for 3 minutes.
4. Using a slotted spoon, place chicken in ungreased air fryer basket. Do not discard excess marinade. Cook chicken for 6 minutes. Shake basket and pour remaining marinade over chicken. Cook for an additional 5 minutes. Using a meat thermometer, ensure internal temperature is at least 75°C.
5. **To assemble:** Serve chicken warm over steamed cauliflower in a large serving dish. Garnish with spring onions, pickled cucumbers and sesame seeds.

PER SERVING

KILOJOULES: 1271 | **FAT:** 8g | **PROTEIN:** 41g | **SODIUM:** 628mg | **FIBRE:** 5g | **CARBOHYDRATES:** 15g | **NET CARBOHYDRATES:** 8g | **SUGAR:** 4g

Chicken Salad with Strawberries and Pecans

Whether you serve this on bread, in lettuce wraps or straight off the spoon, the strawberries add such a fresh twist on this classic salad. The crunch from the pecans gives a textural element that adds another welcome surprise!

Hands-On Time: 10 minutes
Cook Time: 18 minutes

Serves 4

2 (230 gram) boneless, skinless chicken breasts, cut into 3cm cubes
1 teaspoon salt
1/4 teaspoon freshly ground black pepper
3/4 cup mayonnaise
3/4 tablespoon fresh lime juice
1/2 cup chopped pecans
1/2 cup finely chopped celery
1/2 cup hulled and diced strawberries

1 Preheat air fryer at 180°C for 3 minutes.
2 Season chicken with salt and pepper.
3 Add chicken cubes in two batches to air fryer basket. Cook for 4 minutes. Shake gently and flip chicken. Cook for an additional 5 minutes. Check the chicken using a meat thermometer to ensure the internal temperature is at least 75°C.
4 Transfer to a plate and cool.
5 Chop chicken and add to a medium bowl. Add remaining ingredients and combine well. Refrigerate covered until ready to eat.

PER SERVING

KILOJOULES: 2184 | **FAT:** 44g | **PROTEIN:** 27g | **SODIUM:** 906mg | **FIBRE:** 2g | **CARBOHYDRATES:** 5g | **NET CARBOHYDRATES:** 3g | **SUGAR:** 2g

Seasoned Chicken Legs

Keep the skin on the chicken legs — not only is it delicious, but it will hold the seasoning better and crisp up in the air fryer. Sooo tasty!

Hands-On Time: 10 minutes
Cook Time: 36 minutes

Serves 4

1 teaspoon baking powder
1 teaspoon dried mustard
1 teaspoon smoked paprika
1 teaspoon garlic powder
1 teaspoon salt
1 teaspoon freshly ground black pepper
680 grams (approximately 6) chicken legs
2 ¼ tablespoons butter, melted

1. Preheat air fryer at 190°C for 3 minutes.
2. In a large bowl, combine baking powder, dried mustard, paprika, garlic powder, salt and pepper. Add chicken and toss until coated.
3. Add half of chicken to air fryer basket lightly greased with olive oil and cook for 10 minutes.
4. Brush chicken lightly with melted butter, then flip and brush other side. Cook for an additional 8 minutes. Using a meat thermometer, ensure internal temperature is at least 75°C.
5. Transfer chicken to a large serving plate and let rest for 5 minutes. Repeat cooking with remaining chicken and serve warm.

PER SERVING

KILOJOULES: 1029 | **FAT:** 17g | **PROTEIN:** 21g | **SODIUM:** 760mg | **FIBRE:** 0g | **CARBOHYDRATES:** 2g | **NET CARBOHYDRATES:** 1g | **SUGAR:** 0g

Yoghurt Curry Chicken Legs

This Indian-inspired dish may be limited in ingredients, but it's overflowing with flavours. The fragrant, richly spiced tomato sauce coats the mild taste of chicken. It is an easy dish to make at home.

Hands-On Time: 10 minutes
Cook Time: 36 minutes

Serves 4

3/4 cup plain Greek yoghurt
3/4 tablespoon no-sugar-added tomato paste
2 teaspoons curry powder
1 teaspoon salt
680 grams (approximately 6) chicken legs
1 1/2 tablespoons chopped fresh mint

1. In a medium bowl, whisk together yoghurt, tomato paste, curry powder and salt. Divide mixture in half. Cover half and place in refrigerator. Add chicken to other half and toss until coated. Cover and refrigerate for 30 minutes up to overnight.
2. Preheat air fryer at 190°C for 3 minutes.
3. Shake excess marinade from chicken. Add half of chicken to air fryer basket lightly greased with olive oil and cook for 10 minutes.
4. Brush chicken lightly with extra yoghurt mixture. Flip and brush other side. Cook for an additional 8 minutes. Using a meat thermometer, ensure internal temperature is at least 75°C.
5. Transfer chicken to a large serving plate and let rest for 5 minutes. Repeat cooking with remaining chicken and serve warm garnished with mint.

PER SERVING

KILOJOULES: 1246 | **FAT:** 15g | **PROTEIN:** 34g | **SODIUM:** 455mg | **FIBRE:** 0g | **CARBOHYDRATES:** 6g | **NET CARBOHYDRATES:** 6g | **SUGAR:** 6g

Garlic Parmie Wings

If you use your air fryer for only one food, make it chicken wings! The convection heat cooks up that chicken skin from all sides, making each bite equally crispy on the outside and juicy on the inside.

Hands-On Time: 10 minutes
Cook Time: 22 minutes

Serves 4

- **3/4 tablespoon water**
- **910 grams chicken wings, split at the joint**
- **1 1/2 tablespoons melted butter, divided**
- **1 1/2 tablespoons grated Parmesan cheese**
- **4 cloves garlic, peeled and minced**
- **1/4 teaspoon salt**

HOW TO SEPARATE CHICKEN WINGS

Some butchers will have the wings already broken down for the consumer; however, more often you will have to purchase whole wings. To separate the wing into the different parts, first stretch it out. There will be two cuts to each wing, yielding three parts: the drumette, the wingette and the tip. Using kitchen shears or a sharp knife, cut the wing at each joint.

1. Pour water into bottom of air fryer to ensure minimum smoke from fat drippings. Preheat air fryer at 120°C for 3 minutes.
2. In a large bowl, toss wings in 1 tablespoon butter. Place wings in ungreased air fryer basket and cook for 6 minutes. Flip and cook for an additional 6 minutes.
3. While wings are cooking, combine remaining butter, Parmesan cheese, garlic and salt in a separate large bowl.
4. Raise temperature on air fryer to 200°C. Flip wings and cook for another 5 minutes. Flip once more and cook for 5 more minutes.
5. Transfer to bowl with sauce and toss, then transfer to a large serving plate and serve warm.

PER SERVING

KILOJOULES: 1255 | **FAT:** 22g | **PROTEIN:** 23g | **SODIUM:** 292mg | **FIBRE:** 0g | **CARBOHYDRATES:** 1g | **NET CARBOHYDRATES:** 1g | **SUGAR:** 0g

Cajun Crumbed Drumettes

The drumette is the portion of the chicken wing that looks like a smaller chicken leg. The tanginess of the sour cream added to the thickened cream mimics the traditional buttermilk used in carb-filled breaded drumettes. Paired with the Cajun seasoning, this Southern US dish is over-the-top!

Hands-On Time: 10 minutes
Cook Time: 40 minutes

Serves 4

- **450 grams chicken drumettes**
- **½ cup cassava flour**
- **½ cup thickened cream**
- **½ cup sour cream**
- **½ cup crushed pork rinds**
- **¾ tablespoon Cajun seasoning**
- **1½ tablespoons melted butter**

1. In a large bowl, toss drumettes in cassava flour. Shake away excess flour and set aside.
2. In a medium bowl, whisk together heavy cream and sour cream. In a separate shallow dish, combine pork rinds and Cajun seasoning.
3. Preheat air fryer at 190°C for 3 minutes.
4. Dip floured drumettes in cream mixture. Coat in seasoned pork rinds. Place half of drumettes in air fryer basket lightly greased with olive oil and cook for 12 minutes.
5. Gently flip chicken and brush with 1 tablespoon butter. Cook for an additional 8 minutes. Using a meat thermometer, ensure internal temperature is at least 75°C.
6. Transfer chicken to a large serving plate and let rest for 5 minutes. Repeat cooking with remaining chicken and serve warm.

PER SERVING

KILOJOULES: 2012 | **FAT:** 38g | **PROTEIN:** 23g | **SODIUM:** 174mg | **FIBRE:** 1g | **CARBOHYDRATES:** 13g | **NET CARBOHYDRATES:** 12g | **SUGAR:** 2g

Bangin' Chicken Wings

The air fryer will cook these chicken wings to perfection! Crispy, creamy, sweet and spicy — you'll feel like you're dining out with these restaurant-quality wings.

Hands-On Time: 10 minutes
Cook Time: 22 minutes

Serves 4

1 1/2 tablespoons sesame oil
1/4 teaspoon fish sauce
2 teaspoons coconut aminos
2 teaspoons sambal oelek
1 teaspoon erythritol sweetener
1 teaspoon fresh lime juice
910 grams chicken wings, split at the joint
3/4 tablespoon water

WHAT IS SAMBAL OELEK?

Sambal oelek is an Indonesian chili paste usually containing salt, vinegar and a variety of other spices. Found at major supermarkets, it actually has the same ingredients and heat level as sriracha, but with zero sugars, so it's perfect for a low-carb diet!

1. Combine sesame oil, fish sauce, coconut aminos, sambal oelek, erythritol and lime juice in a medium bowl. Divide mixture in half. Toss wings in half of sauce, cover and refrigerate for 30 minutes. Cover and refrigerate other half.
2. Preheat air fryer at 120°C for 3 minutes. Place water in bottom of air fryer to ensure minimum smoke from fat drippings. Place wings in ungreased air fryer basket and cook for 6 minutes. Flip wings and cook for an additional 6 minutes.
3. Raise temperature on air fryer to 200°C. Flip wings and cook for 5 minutes. Flip wings once more and cook for an additional 5 minutes.
4. Transfer wings to bowl with remaining sauce and toss. Serve.

PER SERVING

KILOJOULES: 1246 | **FAT:** 23g | **PROTEIN:** 22g | **SODIUM:** 178mg | **FIBRE:** 0g | **CARBOHYDRATES:** 2g | **NET CARBOHYDRATES:** 1g | **SUGAR:** 1g

Spicy Yellow Mustard Wings

With a bit of Asian flair, these spicy wings are screaming to be eaten with friends alongside a few cold brews. Double or triple this recipe depending on the size of your group!

Hands-On Time: 10 minutes
Cook Time: 22 minutes

Serves 4

- **3/4 tablespoon water**
- **2 pounds chicken wings, split at the joint**
- **3/4 tablespoon sesame oil**
- **1 1/2 tablespoons spicy yellow mustard**
- **3/4 tablespoon coconut aminos**
- **1 teaspoon erythritol sweetener**
- **1 teaspoon apple cider vinegar**

1. Preheat air fryer at 120°C for 3 minutes. Pour water in bottom of air fryer to ensure minimum smoke from fat drippings.
2. In a large bowl, toss wings in sesame oil. Place in ungreased air fryer basket and cook for 6 minutes. Flip wings and cook for an additional 6 minutes.
3. While wings are cooking, combine mustard, coconut aminos, erythritol and apple cider vinegar in a separate large bowl.
4. Raise temperature on air fryer to 200°C. Flip wings and cook for 5 minutes. Flip again and cook for an additional 5 minutes.
5. Transfer wings to bowl with sauce and toss. Serve.

PER SERVING

KILOJOULES: 1138 | **FAT:** 19g | **PROTEIN:** 22g | **SODIUM:** 253mg | **FIBRE:** 0g | **CARBOHYDRATES:** 2g | **NET CARBOHYDRATES:** 1g | **SUGAR:** 1g

Cheesy Chicken Patties

The addition of onion and cheese in this recipe lends a moistness and creaminess to counter the low-fat meat, and it gives a flavour that blends well with the simply seasoned salt and pepper.

Hands-On Time: 10 minutes
Cook Time: 26 minutes

Serves 4

- 450 grams chicken mince
- 1 ½ tablespoons peeled and diced brown onion
- ¼ cup shredded Cheddar cheese
- ¼ cup chopped fresh parsley
- 1 large egg white, beaten
- ¼ teaspoon salt
- ¼ teaspoon freshly ground black pepper

1. Preheat air fryer at 180°C for 3 minutes.
2. In a large bowl, combine all ingredients and form into four patties, making a slight indentation in the middle of each patty. (Patties tend to puff up in the middle during the cooking process, so making an indentation will ensure the patty doesn't become a meatball.)
3. Add two patties to air fryer basket lightly greased with olive oil and cook for 6 minutes. Flip patties and cook for an additional 7 minutes, until internal temperature is at least 75°C. Transfer cooked patties to a large serving plate and repeat cooking with remaining patties.
4. Serve warm.

PER SERVING

KILOJOULES: 832 | **FAT:** 12g | **PROTEIN:** 22g | **SODIUM:** 276mg | **FIBRE:** 0g | **CARBOHYDRATES:** 1g | **NET CARBOHYDRATES:** 1g | **SUGAR:** 0g

Chicken and Goat Cheese Balls

Ground chicken can be a bit dry, but with the addition of the onion and goat cheese, these lean, mean chicken and goat cheese balls are just what the doctor ordered!

Hands-On Time: 10 minutes
Cook Time: 24 minutes

Serves 4

- 450 grams chicken mince
- 1 1/2 tablespoons peeled and grated brown onion
- 1/4 cup chopped fresh basil leaves
- 1/3 cup goat cheese crumbled
- 1/2 cup ground pork rinds
- 1/2 teaspoon garlic powder

1. Preheat air fryer at 180°C for 3 minutes.
2. In a large bowl, combine all ingredients and form into 18 meatballs, about 2 tablespoons each.
3. Add 9 balls to air fryer basket lightly greased with olive oil. Cook for 6 minutes. Shake basket and cook for an additional 6 minutes.
4. Transfer cooked balls to a serving plate and repeat cooking with remaining 9 balls. Serve warm.

PER SERVING

KILOJOULES: 962 | **FAT:** 14g | **PROTEIN:** 25g | **SODIUM:** 192mg | **FIBRE:** 0g | **CARBOHYDRATES:** 1g | **NET CARBOHYDRATES:** 1g | **SUGAR:** 0g

Salsa Chicken

This is absolutely the easiest, tastiest and lowest-calorie meal you can prepare in minutes on the hour. Trust your own heat-o-meter when choosing your salsa or make some fruit salsas instead.

Hands-On Time: 5 minutes
Cook Time: 30 minutes

Serves 2

- 450 grams (approximately 4) boneless, skinless chicken thighs
- 1 cup mild chunky salsa

1. Preheat air fryer at 180°C for 3 minutes.
2. Place chicken thighs in square cake barrel. Cover with salsa.
3. Cook for 30 minutes. Using a meat thermometer, ensure the chicken is at least 75°C. Cook for another minute if necessary.
4. Transfer to a serving plate and let rest for 5 minutes. Serve warm.

PER SERVING

KILOJOULES: 1292 | **FAT:** 6g | **PROTEIN:** 53g | **SODIUM:** 1,012mg | **FIBRE:** 2g | **CARBOHYDRATES:** 8g | **NET CARBOHYDRATES:** 6g | **SUGAR:** 5g

Barbecue Chicken Meatballs

These delectable meatballs are filled with barbecue flavour down to the pork rinds. If you can't get your hands on barbecue-flavoured pork rinds, just substitute the plain variety — they will still work. Also, add a little cayenne pepper to the mix if you like the heat!

Hands-On Time: 10 minutes
Cook Time: 16 minutes

Serves 4

450 grams chicken mince
1 large egg
½ cup crushed barbecue-flavoured pork rinds
¾ tablespoon sour cream
2 teaspoons brown mustard
1 ½ tablespoons peeled and grated brown onion
1 ½ tablespoons no-added-sugar tomato paste
1 teaspoon ground cumin
1 teaspoon chilli powder

1. Preheat air fryer at 180°C for 3 minutes.
2. Combine all ingredients in a large bowl. Form into 18 meatballs, about 2 tablespoons each.
3. Add half of meatballs to air fryer basket lightly greased with olive oil and cook for 6 minutes. Shake basket and cook for an additional 2 minutes.
4. Transfer cooked meatballs to a large serving dish and repeat cooking with remaining meatballs. Serve warm.

PER SERVING

KILOJOULES: 904 | **FAT:** 13g | **PROTEIN:** 24g | **SODIUM:** 208mg | **FIBRE:** 1g | **CARBOHYDRATES:** 2g | **NET CARBOHYDRATES:** 1g | **SUGAR:** 1g

Strawberry Basil-Glazed Chicken Tenders

Sweet and savoury *and* salty — yes please! This is the chicken meal your kids will scream for more of. Switch up your flavours by experimenting with different herbs and the variety of sugar-free jams and preserves available!

Hands-On Time: 10 minutes
Cook Time: 9 minutes

Serves 4

1/4 cup sugar-reduced strawberry jam
2 1/4 tablespoons chopped fresh basil, divided
1 teaspoon pulp-free orange juice
1/4 teaspoon salt
1/4 teaspoon freshly ground black pepper
450 grams chicken tenderloins

1. In a medium bowl, combine preserves, 2 tablespoons basil, orange juice, jam and pepper. Add chicken. Cover and refrigerate for 30 minutes up to overnight.
2. Preheat air fryer at 180°C for 3 minutes.
3. Add chicken to ungreased air fryer basket and cook for 4 minutes. Shake gently and flip chicken. Cook for an additional 5 minutes. Using a meat thermometer, ensure internal temperature is at least 75°C.
4. Transfer chicken to a large serving plate and let rest for 5 minutes, then garnish with remaining basil and serve warm.

PER SERVING

KILOJOULES: 720 | **FAT:** 3g | **PROTEIN:** 26g | **SODIUM:** 196mg | **FIBRE:** 0g | **CARBOHYDRATES:** 13g | **NET CARBOHYDRATES:** 1g | **SUGAR:** 1g

WHAT IS A CHICKEN TENDERLOIN?

You can generally find ready-to-eat chicken tenderloins already cut in the frozen chicken section. If not, just cut 3cm slices from a chicken breast — it's the same thing. Also, you can often save a few bucks by cutting your own!

Chicken Ratatouille Stir-Fry

Ratatouille is a French stewed dish with tomatoes, eggplant, zucchini and capsicum. This air fryer version with chicken gives you a full meal in just minutes, much less time than the traditional stew would take to make.

Hands-On Time: 15 minutes
Cook Time: 15 minutes

Serves 4

- 450 grams boneless, skinless chicken thighs, cut into 3cm cubes
- 1 small eggplant, cut into 3cm cubes
- 1 medium zucchini, cut into 3cm cubes
- 1 small yellow bell capsicum, seeded and diced
- 1 teaspoon salt
- 1 teaspoon Italian seasoning
- 1 ½ tablespoons olive oil
- 410 grams canned diced tomatoes, including juice
- 1 ½ tablespoons grated Parmesan cheese
- 1 ½ tablespoons julienned fresh basil leaves

1. Preheat air fryer at 200°C for 3 minutes.
2. In a large bowl, combine chicken, eggplant, zucchini, capsicum, salt, Italian seasoning and olive oil.
3. Add chicken and vegetables to ungreased air fryer basket and cook for 7 minutes.
4. Transfer chicken mixture to an ungreased cake barrel. Stir in tomatoes with juice. Cook for an additional 8 minutes. Using a meat thermometer, ensure internal temperature is at least 75°C.
5. Transfer to a large serving dish. Toss with Parmesan cheese and garnish with basil. Serve.

PER SERVING

KILOJOULES: 1033 | **FAT:** 12g | **PROTEIN:** 25g | **SODIUM:** 843mg | **FIBRE:** 3g | **CARBOHYDRATES:** 7g | **NET CARBOHYDRATES:** 5g | **SUGAR:** 5g

Sweet and Spicy Chicken Bites

Serve this sweet and spicy dish as is, over cauliflower rice or in lettuce wraps. In addition, you can serve it up in takeout boxes purchased online or in most craft stores — just don't forget the chopsticks to round out the experience!

Hands-On Time: 15 minutes
Cook Time: 15 minutes

Serves 4

- 1 large egg
- 1 teaspoon water
- 3 tablespoons arrowroot flour
- 450 grams boneless, skinless chicken thighs, cut into 3cm cubes
- 1 teaspoon sesame oil
- 2 teaspoons apple cider vinegar
- 2 tablespoons coconut aminos
- 3 cloves garlic, peeled and minced
- 2 teaspoons peeled and grated fresh ginger
- 2 teaspoons chilli garlic sauce
- 2 teaspoons erythritol sweetener
- 1/4 teaspoon salt
- 1/4 teaspoon freshly ground white pepper
- 1 spring onion, thinly sliced at a diagonal

1. Preheat air fryer at 200°C for 3 minutes.
2. In a medium bowl, whisk together egg, water and arrowroot flour. Add chicken pieces and toss until fully coated.
3. In a large bowl, whisk together sesame oil, apple cider vinegar, coconut aminos, garlic, ginger, chilli garlic sauce, erythritol, salt and pepper. Set aside.
4. Add chicken to air fryer basket lightly greased with olive oil and cook for 15 minutes, flipping chicken every 5 minutes.
5. Transfer cooked chicken to bowl with marinade and gently toss to coat.
6. Transfer to a large serving plate, garnish with green onion, and serve.

PER SERVING

KILOJOULES: 875 | **FAT:** 7g | **PROTEIN:** 24g | **SODIUM:** 408mg | **FIBRE:** 1g | **CARBOHYDRATES:** 12g | **NET CARBOHYDRATES:** 10g | **SUGAR:** 2g

Chicken Fajita Bowl

Move over, crunchy taco shells, we don't need you anymore. This complete fajita bowl is bursting with Mexican flavours — without the carb explosion usually associated with Taco Tuesday.

Hands-On Time: 15 minutes
Cook Time: 16 minutes

Serves 4

- ¾ tablespoon olive oil
- 2 teaspoons arrowroot flour
- ¼ teaspoon chilli powder
- ¼ teaspoon salt
- ¼ teaspoon smoked paprika
- ¼ teaspoon ground cumin
- ½ teaspoon erythritol sweetener
- ⅛ teaspoon onion powder
- ⅛ teaspoon garlic powder
- 450 grams boneless, skinless chicken breasts, cut into 8cm long strips
- 4 medium Roma tomatoes, cored, seeded and diced
- 1 medium jalapeño, sliced and seeded
- ¼ cup peeled and diced red onion
- ½ cup Mexican blend cheese
- 3 tablespoons sour cream
- 1 medium avocado, peeled, pitted and diced

1. In a large bowl, whisk together olive oil, arrowroot flour, chilli powder, salt, paprika, cumin, erythritol, onion powder and garlic powder. Add chicken strips and toss. Refrigerate covered for 30 minutes up to overnight.
2. Preheat air fryer at 200°C for 3 minutes.
3. Add half of chicken to ungreased air fryer basket and cook for 4 minutes. Shake basket. Cook for an additional 4 minutes. Using a meat thermometer, ensure internal temperature is at least 75°C.
4. Transfer cooked chicken to two medium bowls and repeat cooking with remaining chicken.
5. Transfer remaining chicken to two more medium bowls. Add tomatoes, jalapeño, red onion, cheese, sour cream and avocado to bowls. Serve.

PER SERVING

KILOJOULES: 1460 | **FAT:** 20g | **PROTEIN:** 31g | **SODIUM:** 330mg | **FIBRE:** 5g | **CARBOHYDRATES:** 13g | **NET CARBOHYDRATES:** 7g | **SUGAR:** 5g

PICKLED JALAPEÑO SLICES

Pickled jalapeño slices would be a great accent to this dish. Just slice and seed a large jalapeño and add to a small bowl with 2 tablespoons apple cider vinegar, 1 tablespoon warm water and 1 teaspoon granular erythritol. Drain the liquid when ready to add to your dish.

Grilled Chicken Cobb Salad

Whether you are looking for lunch or dinner, this salad is stocked with delicious fillers, making it a complete meal. Also, if you have leftover chicken from the beginning of the week, use it up in this easy-to-put-together salad!

Hands-On Time: 10 minutes
Cook Time: 18 minutes

Serves 4

- **2 (230 gram) boneless, skinless chicken breasts, cut into 3cm cubes**
- **1 tablespoon avocado oil**
- **½ teaspoon salt**
- **¼ teaspoon freshly ground black pepper**
- **4 cups chopped cos lettuce**
- **1 ½ tablespoons olive oil**
- **¾ tablespoon fresh lemon juice**
- **2 Air-Fried Hard-"Boiled" Eggs, sliced (see recipe on page 16)**
- **4 pieces sugar-free bacon, cooked and crumbled**
- **2 medium Roma tomatoes, cored, seeded and diced**
- **¼ cup blue cheese crumbled**
- **¼ cup peeled and diced red onion**
- **1 large avocado, peeled, pitted and diced**

1. Preheat air fryer at 180°C for 3 minutes.
2. In a large bowl, toss chicken cubes with avocado oil. Season with salt and pepper.
3. Add half of chicken cubes to ungreased air fryer basket. Cook for 4 minutes. Shake gently and flip chicken. Cook for an additional 5 minutes. Using a meat thermometer, ensure internal temperature is at least 75°C.
4. Transfer cooked chicken to a large plate. Repeat cooking with remaining chicken.
5. In a separate large bowl, toss cos lettuce with olive oil and lemon juice. Distribute into four medium bowls.
6. Garnish salads with remaining ingredients, including cooked chicken. Serve.

PER SERVING

KILOJOULES: 1786 | **FAT:** 28g | **PROTEIN:** 35g | **SODIUM:** 632mg | **FIBRE:** 5g | **CARBOHYDRATES:** 9g | **NET CARBOHYDRATES:** 5g | **SUGAR:** 3g

Dilly Chicken Salad

This is the perfect meal to make and take along for a family outing — just stow beside a frozen ice pack and then enjoy this fresh meal out in nature!

Hands-On Time: 10 minutes
Cook Time: 18 minutes

Serves 4

- **2 (230 gram) boneless, skinless chicken breasts, cut into 3cm cubes**
- **½ teaspoon salt**
- **¼ teaspoon freshly ground black pepper**
- **¾ cup mayonnaise**
- **¾ tablespoon fresh lime juice**
- **1½ tablespoons chopped fresh dill**
- **½ cup halved seedless red grapes**
- **½ cup finely chopped celery**
- **1 medium shallot, peeled and diced**

1. Preheat air fryer at 180°C for 3 minutes.
2. Season chicken with salt and pepper. Add half of chicken cubes to ungreased air fryer basket. Cook for 4 minutes. Shake gently and flip chicken. Cook for an additional 5 minutes. Using a meat thermometer, ensure internal temperature is at least 75°C.
3. Transfer cooked chicken to a large plate. Repeat cooking with remaining chicken.
4. Toss chicken into a large serving bowl with remaining ingredients. Refrigerate covered for 1 hour up to overnight until ready to eat.

PER SERVING

KILOJOULES: 1840 | **FAT:** 34g | **PROTEIN:** 26g | **SODIUM:** 616mg | **FIBRE:** 1g | **CARBOHYDRATES:** 6g | **NET CARBOHYDRATES:** 5g | **SUGAR:** 4g

Tandoori-Inspired Chicken Kebabs

These beautifully spiced Indian chicken kebabs are excellent served over some steamed riced cauliflower or in lettuce wraps with some homemade sugar-free chutney. Have fun incorporating the chicken into your own creations.

Hands-On Time: 15 minutes
Cook Time: 24 minutes

Serves 4

- 1 small brown onion, peeled and diced
- 1 (5cm) knob fresh ginger, peeled and minced
- 1 ½ tablespoons fresh lime juice
- 1 cup canned unsweetened coconut milk
- 1 ½ tablespoons no-added-sugar tomato paste
- 1 ½ tablespoons olive oil
- ¾ tablespoon ground cumin
- ¾ tablespoon ground coriander
- 1 teaspoon cayenne pepper
- 1 teaspoon ground turmeric
- 2 teaspoons salt
- 450 grams boneless, skinless chicken thighs, cut into 3cm cubes
- 1 ½ tablespoons chopped fresh mint leaves

1. In a medium bowl, combine all ingredients except chicken and mint leaves. Add chicken pieces and toss until fully coated. Refrigerate covered for 2 hours up to overnight.
2. Preheat air fryer at 180°C for 3 minutes.
3. Skewer chicken on eight skewers and place half of skewers on a kebab rack. Place rack in air fryer basket and cook for 12 minutes. Discard marinade.
4. Transfer cooked kebabs to a large serving dish. Repeat cooking with remaining skewers. Garnish with mint leaves and serve.

PER SERVING

KILOJOULES: 627 | **FAT:** 4g | **PROTEIN:** 26g | **SODIUM:** 402mg | **FIBRE:** 0g | **CARBOHYDRATES:** 1g | **NET CARBOHYDRATES:** 1g | **SUGAR:** 0g

Honey Mustard Chicken Skewers

Chicken, vegetables and honey mustard: who needs a drive-through when this healthy, delicious meal can be ready in about 30 minutes with minimal prep.

Hands-On Time: 10 minutes
Cook Time: 24 minutes

Serves 4

450 grams boneless, skinless chicken thighs, cut into 3cm cubes
½ cup Low-Carb Honey Mustard (see recipe on page 62)
½ medium red onion, peeled and chopped into 3cm pieces
1 medium green capsicum, seeded and chopped into 3cm pieces
1½ tablespoons chopped fresh parsley

1 In a medium bowl, combine chicken cubes and honey mustard. Refrigerate covered for 30 minutes.
2 Preheat air fryer at 180°C for 3 minutes.
3 Skewer chicken and vegetables alternately on eight skewers and place half of skewers on a kebab rack. Place rack in air fryer basket and cook for 12 minutes.
4 Transfer cooked kebabs to a large serving dish. Repeat cooking with remaining skewers. Garnish with fresh parsley and serve warm.

PER SERVING

KILOJOULES: 1083 | **FAT:** 15g | **PROTEIN:** 26g | **SODIUM:** 271mg | **FIBRE:** 1g | **CARBOHYDRATES:** 7g | **NET CARBOHYDRATES:** 3g | **SUGAR:** 2g

Dijon "Maple"-Glazed Chook

Just a touch of the maple extract, which can be found next to the vanilla extract in most grocery stores, is all you need to trick your taste buds into thinking you've added some thick maple syrup to your mustard.

Hands-On Time: 10 minutes
Cook Time: 28 minutes

Serves 2

- 1 1/2 tablespoons butter, melted
- 1 1/2 tablespoons Dijon mustard
- 1/2 teaspoon salt
- 1/2 teaspoon freshly ground black pepper
- 1/8 teaspoon ground nutmeg
- 1/2 teaspoon erythritol sweetener
- 1/8 teaspoon maple extract
- 1 tablespoon olive oil
- 1 (approximately 1.2kg) whole chicken
- 1 small clementine mandarin, quartered

1. Preheat air fryer at 180°C for 3 minutes.
2. In a small bowl, combine butter, mustard, salt, pepper, nutmeg, erythritol and maple extract.
3. Rub oil over and inside chicken. Sprinkle chicken with seasoning mixture. Stuff clementine into the chicken's cavity.
4. Place chicken in ungreased air fryer basket. Cook for 10 minutes. Flip chicken. Cook for another 10 minutes. Flip chicken and cook for an additional 8 minutes. Using a meat thermometer, ensure internal temperature is at least 75°C.
5. Transfer chicken to a cutting board and let rest for 5 minutes. Once cool enough to handle, split in half by cutting down the spine. Serve warm.

PER SERVING

KILOJOULES: 2271 | **FAT:** 43g | **PROTEIN:** 30g | **SODIUM:** 1,029mg | **FIBRE:** 1g | **CARBOHYDRATES:** 6g | **NET CARBOHYDRATES:** 4g | **SUGAR:** 3g

6

Beef and Pork Main Dishes

Naturally low-carb, beef and pork crisp up nicely in the air fryer and make fantastic additions to your low-carb diet. Packing tons of protein and naturally healthy fats, two of the three macronutrients your body needs to survive, these are two foods you won't want to skip over. And thanks to the air fryer, you have dozens of easy, delicious options for both!

With recipes ranging from Strip Steak with Mushrooms and Onions and Chopped Steakhouse Salad to Inside Out Barbecue Sliders and Buffalo-Style Pork Meatballs, this chapter will help get you started on some classic air fryer beef and pork recipes, and also introduce you to some soon-to-be favourites. Enjoy!

Strip Steak with Mushrooms and Onions

This recipe is so simple but so exquisite. The steak seasons the vegetables while cooking, lending an earthy and salty flavour to the mushrooms and onions. The cooking time yields a medium-rare steak, so adjust for your preferred level of cooking.

Hands-On Time: 5 minutes
Cook Time: 9 minutes

Serves 2

3/4 tablespoon olive oil
230 grams sliced white mushrooms
1/2 medium brown onion, peeled and sliced into half-moons
1/8 teaspoon plus 1/2 teaspoon salt, divided
1 (340 gram) strip steak
1/2 teaspoon smoked paprika
1/4 teaspoon freshly ground black pepper

1. Preheat air fryer at 200°C for 3 minutes.
2. In a medium bowl, toss together olive oil, mushrooms, onion and 1/8 teaspoon salt. Place in an even layer in ungreased air fryer basket.
3. Season steak with remaining 1/2 teaspoon salt, paprika and pepper. Place steak on top of mushroom mixture.
4. Cook for 5 minutes, then flip steak and cook for an additional 4 minutes.
5. Transfer steak to a cutting board and let rest for 5 minutes, then cut in half. Place steak, mushrooms and onions on two large plates and serve warm.

PER SERVING

KILOJOULES: 1301 | **FAT:** 15g | **PROTEIN:** 37g | **SODIUM:** 803mg | **FIBRE:** 2g | **CARBOHYDRATES:** 7g | **NET CARBOHYDRATES:** 5g | **SUGAR:** 3g

T-Bone with Garlic Rosemary Compound Butter

Compound butter is a just a fancy way to say butter with add-ins. If you've never experienced this little delicacy, start adding it to your steaks. It is so easy to make and lends so much flavour to your meal. You'll never go back!

Hands-On Time: 10 minutes
Cook Time: 10 minutes

Serves 2

- **1 ½ tablespoons butter, softened**
- **¼ teaspoon lemon juice**
- **2 cloves garlic, peeled and minced**
- **1 teaspoon minced fresh rosemary**
- **1 (570 gram, 7cm-thick) T-bone steak, fat trimmed, leaving a 6mm ribbon**
- **1 teaspoon salt**
- **½ teaspoon freshly ground black pepper**
- **1 ½ tablespoons water**

1. Combine butter, lemon juice, garlic and rosemary in a small bowl. Transfer butter onto baking paper or plastic wrap. Roll into a log, spinning ends to tighten. Refrigerate for 2 hours up to overnight.
2. Remove T-bone from refrigerator for 30 minutes before cooking. Season with salt and pepper.
3. Preheat air fryer at 200°F for 3 minutes. Add 2 tablespoons water to air fryer.
4. Place steak in air fryer basket lightly greased with olive oil. Cook for 5 minutes. Flip steak and cook for an additional 5 minutes until a meat thermometer ensures an internal temperature of at least 63°C, or until cooked to your liking.
5. Transfer steak to a cutting board and let rest for 5 minutes. Slice butter and add to top of steak. Let melt over meat. Serve warm.

PER SERVING

KILOJOULES: 2623 | **FAT:** 48g | **PROTEIN:** 45g | **SODIUM:** 1,276mg | **FIBRE:** 0g | **CARBOHYDRATES:** 2g | **NET CARBOHYDRATES:** 1g | **SUGAR:** 0g

PRETTY COMPOUND BUTTER MOULDS

If you are wanting to display your butter in a better way than rolling it up in plastic wrap and forming a log, actual butter moulds can be purchased online. Alternatively, you can use silicone chocolate moulds that come in all sorts of shapes and sizes and can be used for different celebrations!

Greek Steak Bowls

The incredible spice blend and straight-out-of-the-air-fryer warmth of this steak plays nicely with the cooled nature of the vegetables and fetta. In less than 15 minutes, you'll be dining exquisitely!

Hands-On Time: 5 minutes
Cook Time: 9 minutes

Serves 2

1 large continental cucumber, diced
2 medium Roma tomatoes, cored, seeded and diced
3/4 tablespoon apple cider vinegar
1 1/2 teaspoons olive oil
5 kalamata olives, pitted and halved
1/4 cup fetta cheese crumbled
1/2 teaspoon dried oregano
1/2 teaspoon dried dill
1/4 teaspoon ground cinnamon
1/4 teaspoon garlic powder
1/8 teaspoon ground nutmeg
1/2 teaspoon salt
1/4 teaspoon freshly ground black pepper
1 (340 gram) strip steak

1. Combine cucumber, tomatoes, apple cider vinegar and olive oil in a medium bowl. Toss in olives and fetta. Refrigerate covered until ready to use.
2. Preheat air fryer at 200°C for 3 minutes.
3. In a small bowl, combine oregano, dill, cinnamon, garlic powder, nutmeg, salt and pepper. Season steak with mixture.
4. Place steak in air fryer basket lightly greased with olive oil. Cook for 5 minutes, then flip steak and cook for an additional 4 minutes or until cooked to your liking.
5. Transfer steak to a cutting board and let rest for 5 minutes, then thinly slice against the grain and distribute between two medium bowls. Top with cucumber mixture and serve.

PER SERVING

KILOJOULES: 1615 | **FAT:** 20g | **PROTEIN:** 38g | **SODIUM:** 1,033mg | **FIBRE:** 3g | **CARBOHYDRATES:** 14g | **NET CARBOHYDRATES:** 11g | **SUGAR:** 7g

Filet Mignon Steaks

There is nothing simple about filet mignon, so all you need is salt and pepper to let the natural flavours shine through. Don't forget to rest the meat before cutting, as this allows the juices to settle back into the meat rather than drip out onto the cutting board.

Hands-On Time: 15 minutes
Cook Time: 12 minutes

Serves 2

2 (230 gram, 14cm thick) filet mignon steaks
1 teaspoon salt
½ teaspoon freshly ground black pepper
¾ tablespoon unsalted butter, cut into 2 pats

1. Preheat air fryer at 190°C for 3 minutes.
2. Season steaks on both sides with salt and pepper. Place in air fryer basket lightly greased with olive oil and cook for 4 minutes. Flip and cook for an additional 4 minutes. Flip one more time and cook for an additional 4 minutes to yield a medium-rare steak.
3. Transfer steaks to a cutting board and top each with 1 pat butter. Let rest for 5 minutes before serving.

PER SERVING

KILOJOULES: 1543 | **FAT:** 19g | **PROTEIN:** 46g | **SODIUM:** 1,258mg | **FIBRE:** 0g | **CARBOHYDRATES:** 1g | **NET CARBOHYDRATES:** 0g | **SUGAR:** 0g

Flank Steak with Creamy Horseradish Sauce

Flank steak is one of the most under-utilised cuts of beef because of its inexpensive nature, yet it rivals the tenderness of filet mignon if cut against the grain. The cool and creamy horseradish sauce adds a little kick to the steak.

Hands-On Time: 10 minutes
Cook Time: 9 minutes

Serves 2

For Creamy Horseradish Sauce

- 1 ½ tablespoons prepared horseradish
- 1 ½ tablespoons plain Greek yoghurt
- 1 ½ tablespoons mayonnaise
- ¾ tablespoon fresh lemon juice
- ⅛ teaspoon salt
- ⅛ teaspoon freshly ground black pepper
- ½ teaspoon Worcestershire sauce

For Flank Steak

- 1 (340 gram) flank steak, cut in half
- 1 ½ tablespoons olive oil
- 1 teaspoon salt
- ½ teaspoon freshly ground black pepper

1. **To make Creamy Horseradish Sauce:** Whisk together all ingredients in a small bowl and refrigerate covered until ready to use.
2. **To make Flank Steak:** Preheat air fryer at 200°C for 3 minutes.
3. Rub flank steak halves with olive oil. Season with salt and pepper.
4. Place steaks in ungreased air fryer basket. Cook for 4 minutes. Flip and cook for an additional 5 minutes or until it is cooked to your liking.
5. Transfer steaks to a cutting board and let rest for 5 minutes, then thinly slice against the grain and place on two medium plates.
6. Drizzle horseradish sauce over steaks and serve immediately.

PER SERVING

KILOJOULES: 2008 | **FAT:** 35g | **PROTEIN:** 36g | **SODIUM:** 1,547mg | **FIBRE:** 1g | **CARBOHYDRATES:** 5g | **NET CARBOHYDRATES:** 4g | **SUGAR:** 2g

Peach Barbecue Pork Chops

Fruit pairs so nicely with pork chops, and this recipe won't let you down. The air fryer sears all sides of the chops while keeping the inside juicy! When choosing sugar-reduced jam, read the labels, as some have hidden ingredients. Do a quick online search for "keto-accepted jam" for a rundown of good options.

Hands-On Time: 5 minutes
Cook Time: 12 minutes

Serves 2

1 ½ tablespoons sugar-reduced peach preserves
1 ½ tablespoons no-added-sugar tomato paste
¾ tablespoon Dijon mustard
1 teaspoon Worcestershire sauce
¾ tablespoon fresh lemon juice
¾ tablespoon olive oil
2 cloves garlic, peeled and minced
2 (3cm-thick) bone-in pork chops

1. In a medium bowl, whisk together peach preserves, tomato paste, Dijon mustard, Worcestershire sauce, lemon juice, olive oil and garlic. Add pork chops to mixture and toss. Refrigerate covered for 30 minutes.
2. Preheat air fryer at 180°C for 3 minutes.
3. Place pork chops in ungreased air fryer basket. Cook for 4 minutes. Flip and cook for 4 more minutes. Flip once more and cook for an additional 4 minutes. Using a meat thermometer, ensure internal temperature is at least 70°C.
4. Transfer pork to a cutting board and let rest for 5 minutes before serving warm.

PER SERVING

KILOJOULES: 1564 | **FAT:** 22g | **PROTEIN:** 28g | **SODIUM:** 277mg | **FIBRE:** 1g | **CARBOHYDRATES:** 18g | **NET CARBOHYDRATES:** 5g | **SUGAR:** 3g

Kickin' Mustard Parmie Pork Chops

The *kickin'* in this recipe is from the horseradish mustard. If a little kick isn't what you like, simply use a Dijon or yellow mustard instead.

Hands-On Time: 5 minutes
Cook Time: 12 minutes

Serves 2

1 large egg white
3/4 tablespoon horseradish mustard
1/2 cup grated Parmesan cheese
1/4 teaspoon freshly ground black pepper
2 (3cm thick) bone-in pork chops
1/4 cup chopped fresh parsley

1. Preheat air fryer at 180°C for 3 minutes.
2. In a small dish, whisk together egg white and horseradish mustard. In a separate small shallow dish, combine Parmesan cheese and black pepper.
3. Dip pork chops in mustard mixture. Coat in Parmesan mixture.
4. Place pork chops in air fryer basket lightly greased with olive oil. Cook for 4 minutes. Flip and cook for 4 minutes, then flip once more and cook for an additional 4 minutes. Using a meat thermometer, ensure the internal temperature is at least 70°C.
5. Transfer pork to a cutting board and let rest for 5 minutes before serving warm. Garnish with parsley.

PER SERVING

KILOJOULES: 1983 | **FAT:** 28g | **PROTEIN:** 51g | **SODIUM:** 543mg | **FIBRE:** 1g | **CARBOHYDRATES:** 2g | **NET CARBOHYDRATES:** 1g | **SUGAR:** 0g

Carne Asada with Salsa Verde

Prep your salsa verde ahead of time and marinate the meat the night before so you are ready to roll when you come home from a busy day. And it can be in your bowl in less than 25 minutes!

Hands-On Time: 10 minutes
Cook Time: 11 minutes

Serves 4

1 (910 gram) flank steak, cut in half
1 ½ cups salsa verde, divided

HOW TO MAKE MEXICAN STYLE SALSA VERDE

The hero ingredient in Mexican Salsa Verde is the Tomatillo. This nightshade looks like a mini green tomato with a husk. Fresh tomatillos are difficult to buy in Australia, but you can grown your own or used the canned variety to make a salsa verde. In a blender, combine 400g of canned tomatillos (drained and rinsed throughly) with ½ onion, 2 garlic cloves, 1 bunch of coriander and 1-3 jalapeños, depending on desired heat. Blend until smooth. Add salt to taste.

1. Place steaks in a large dish with 1 cup salsa verde. Cover and marinate refrigerated for 1 hour up to overnight.
2. Preheat air fryer at 200°C for 3 minutes.
3. Place steaks in air fryer basket lightly greased with olive oil. Cook for 6 minutes. Flip and cook for an additional 5 minutes or until cooked to your liking.
4. Transfer steaks to a cutting board and let rest for 5 minutes, then thinly slice against the grain and transfer to four medium plates. Serve warm with remaining ½ cup salsa verde.

PER SERVING

KILOJOULES: 1363 | **FAT:** 14g | **PROTEIN:** 46g | **SODIUM:** 165mg | **FIBRE:** 1g | **CARBOHYDRATES:** 2g | **NET CARBOHYDRATES:** 2g | **SUGAR:** 1g

Chopped Steakhouse Salad

Although the plain walnuts lend an excellent crunch to this salad, try adding Candied Walnuts (see recipe on page 215) for an extra boost of flavour.

Hands-On Time: 10 minutes
Cook Time: 9 minutes

Serves 2

- **1 ½ tablespoons olive oil**
- **¾ tablespoon apple cider vinegar**
- **¾ tablespoon sour cream**
- **1 teaspoon Dijon mustard**
- **1 (340 gram) strip steak**
- **½ teaspoon salt**
- **¼ teaspoon freshly ground black pepper**
- **1 small head iceberg lettuce, cut into thin strips**
- **1 ½ tablespoons chopped walnuts**
- **¼ cup blue cheese crumbled**
- **4 medium cherry tomatoes, halved**
- **¼ cup fresh blueberries**

1. Whisk together olive oil, apple cider vinegar, sour cream and Dijon mustard in a small bowl. Refrigerate covered until ready to use.
2. Preheat air fryer at 200°C for 3 minutes.
3. Season steak with salt and pepper. Place in air fryer basket lightly greased with olive oil. Cook for 5 minutes, then flip and cook for an additional 4 minutes or until cooked to your liking.
4. Transfer steak to a cutting board and let rest for 5 minutes.
5. Transfer lettuce to a large serving bowl and toss with dressing, then transfer to two medium bowls.
6. Thinly slice steak and add to salads. Garnish with walnuts, blue cheese crumbles, tomatoes and blueberries. Serve.

PER SERVING

KILOJOULES: 2096 | **FAT:** 32g | **PROTEIN:** 41g | **SODIUM:** 937mg | **FIBRE:** 3g | **CARBOHYDRATES:** 12g | **NET CARBOHYDRATES:** 8g | **SUGAR:** 7g

Giant Italian Meatballs

What are better than meatballs? Giant meatballs! The ricotta and Parmesan cheeses lend a creaminess to the dish, while using beef and pork rounds out the flavour profile. And serving it in some napolitana sauce... now that's Italian!

Hands-On Time: 10 minutes
Cook Time: 25 minutes

Serves 4

- 230 grams lean beef mince
- 230 grams pork mince
- 1 large egg, beaten
- 1 1/2 tablespoons no-sugar-added tomato paste
- 1/4 cup ricotta cheese
- 1/3 cup grated Parmesan cheese
- 3 cloves garlic, peeled and minced
- 1/4 cup peeled and grated brown onion
- 1/2 teaspoon salt
- 1/4 teaspoon freshly ground black pepper
- 1/4 cup almond flour
- 1/4 cup chopped fresh parsley
- 2 cups no-sugar-added napolitana sauce

1. Combine all ingredients except for napolitana sauce in a large bowl. Form mixture into four meatballs.
2. Preheat air fryer at 200°C for 3 minutes.
3. Cut a piece of baking paper to fit bottom of air fryer basket. Place meatballs on paper. Cook for 20 minutes.
4. In a medium frying pan, heat sauce over medium heat for 3 minutes. Add cooked meatballs and roll them around in sauce for 2 minutes.
5. Transfer meatballs to a large plate and serve warm with sauce over the top.

PER SERVING

KILOJOULES: 1669 | **FAT:** 25g | **PROTEIN:** 29g | **SODIUM:** 732mg | **FIBRE:** 3g | **CARBOHYDRATES:** 14g | **NET CARBOHYDRATES:** 10g | **SUGAR:** 7g

Juicy Beef Sliders

Who needs the bun when the meat is the star? The grated brown onion lends a moistness to the beef, and no one in the family will even know you snuck it in! The simplicity of the seasoning adds just enough to let the burger shine.

Hands-On Time: 5 minutes
Cook Time: 18 minutes

Serves 4

450 grams lean beef mince
1/3 cup peeled and grated yellow onion
1/2 teaspoon smoked paprika
1/2 teaspoon salt
1/4 teaspoon freshly ground black pepper

1. In a medium bowl, combine all ingredients. Form into eight patties. Make a slight indentation in the middle of each.
2. Preheat air fryer at 180°C for 3 minutes.
3. Place four patties in air fryer basket or on air fryer grill pan lightly greased with olive oil. Cook for 5 minutes. Flip sliders and cook for an additional 4 minutes or until cooked to your liking.
4. Transfer cooked sliders to a large serving plate and repeat cooking with remaining sliders. Serve warm.

PER SERVING

KILOJOULES: 870 | **FAT:** 13g | **PROTEIN:** 20g | **SODIUM:** 345mg | **FIBRE:** 0g | **CARBOHYDRATES:** 1g | **NET CARBOHYDRATES:** 1g | **SUGAR:** 1g

Inside Out Barbecue Sliders

The cheese and bacon are *inside* the meat in this recipe, giving your guests a savoury and cheesy surprise when they bite into these sliders. Change the flavour of the meat by trying different sugar-reduced barbecue sauces.

Hands-On Time: 5 minutes
Cook Time: 18 minutes

Makes 8 sliders

- **230 grams lean beef mince**
- **230 grams pork mince**
- **3/4 tablespoon reduced sugar barbecue sauce**
- **1/2 teaspoon salt**
- **1/4 teaspoon freshly ground black pepper**
- **3 rashers middle bacon, cooked and diced**
- **8 (28 gram) cubes Cheddar cheese**

1. In a medium bowl, combine ground beef, ground pork, barbecue sauce, salt and pepper. Form into eight equal balls.
2. Press your thumb into the centre of each ball. Add bacon bits and Cheddar cheese cubes to hole. Seal.
3. Preheat air fryer at 180°C for 3 minutes.
4. Place four patties in air fryer basket or on air fryer grill pan lightly greased with olive oil. Cook for 5 minutes. Flip sliders and cook for an additional 4 minutes or until cooked to your liking.
5. Transfer cooked sliders to a large plate and repeat cooking with remaining sliders. Serve warm.

PER SERVING (1 SLIDER)

KILOJOULES: 1008 | **FAT:** 18g | **PROTEIN:** 18g | **SODIUM:** 444mg | **FIBRE:** 0g | **CARBOHYDRATES:** 1g | **NET CARBOHYDRATES:** 1g | **SUGAR:** 1g

Dijon Rosemary Pork Loin Roast

This meal is simply seasoned to accent and allow the beautiful pork flavour to shine through. Because the loin roast is a less fatty cut, it is necessary to check the internal temperature toward the end of cooking. If overcooked, the roast can become dry. If cooked correctly, it is heaven!

Hands-On Time: 10 minutes
Cook Time: 40 minutes

Serves 4

- 1 ½ tablespoons Dijon mustard
- 2 teaspoons olive oil
- ½ teaspoon salt
- ¼ teaspoon freshly ground black pepper
- 1 teaspoon dried rosemary
- 1 (910 gram) boneless pork loin roast

1. Preheat air fryer at 180°C for 3 minutes.
2. In a small bowl, whisk together mustard, olive oil, salt, pepper and rosemary. Massage into loin on all sides.
3. Place pork in ungreased air fryer basket. Cook for 20 minutes. Flip and cook for an additional 20 minutes. Using a meat thermometer, ensure internal temperature is at least 70°C.
4. Transfer pork to a cutting board and let rest for 5 minutes before slicing and serving warm.

PER SERVING

KILOJOULES: 1769 | **FAT:** 26g | **PROTEIN:** 42g | **SODIUM:** 546mg | **FIBRE:** 0g | **CARBOHYDRATES:** 0g | **NET CARBOHYDRATES:** 0g | **SUGAR:** 0g

Blackened Pork Tenderloin

Here, *blackened* simply means that the meat has been dipped in butter and sprinkled with herbs and spices. The saltiness from the pork will enhance the other flavours as the air fryer crisps up the exterior.

Hands-On Time: 10 minutes
Cook Time: 16 minutes

Serves 2

- **3/4 tablespoon smoked paprika**
- **2 teaspoons ground cumin**
- **1 teaspoon garlic powder**
- **1 teaspoon onion powder**
- **1/4 teaspoon cayenne pepper**
- **1 teaspoon salt**
- **1/2 teaspoon freshly ground black pepper**
- **1 teaspoon Italian seasoning**
- **1 1/2 tablespoons butter, melted**
- **1 teaspoon Worcestershire sauce**
- **1 (450 gram) pork tenderloin, halved crosswise**

1. Combine paprika, cumin, garlic powder, onion powder, cayenne pepper, salt, black pepper and Italian seasoning in a small bowl. Set aside.
2. Preheat air fryer at 180°C for 3 minutes.
3. Whisk together butter and Worcestershire sauce in a separate small bowl. Brush over pork tenderloin halves. Rub with seasoning mix.
4. Place pork in air fryer basket lightly greased with olive oil. Cook for 8 minutes. Flip. Cook for an additional 8 minutes. Using a meat thermometer, ensure internal temperature is at least 70°C.
5. Transfer pork to a cutting board and let rest for 5 minutes before slicing and serving warm.

PER SERVING

KILOJOULES: 1564 | **FAT:** 18g | **PROTEIN:** 45g | **SODIUM:** 1,295mg | **FIBRE:** 2g | **CARBOHYDRATES:** 6g | **NET CARBOHYDRATES:** 4g | **SUGAR:** 1g

Crispy Pork over Coconut Lime Cauliflower Rice

By thinly slicing the pork prior to cooking, you allow the air fryer to give this succulent meat those delicious crispy edges, which adds another dimension of flavour and texture to the dish.

Hands-On Time: 15 minutes
Cook Time: 25 minutes

Serves 4

For Pork

- 1 1/2 tablespoons avocado oil
- 1 1/2 tablespoons coconut aminos
- 2 teaspoons red chilli paste
- 2 teaspoons yellow mustard
- 2 teaspoons erythritol sweetener
- 1 (450 gram) pork shoulder, trimmed and thinly sliced into 3cm strips
- 1 1/2 tablespoons water

For Cauliflower Rice

- 3/4 tablespoon coconut oil
- 3 cups riced cauliflower
- 6 spring onions, whites and greens separated, divided
- 4 cloves garlic, peeled and minced
- 1 cup canned unsweetened coconut milk
- 3/4 tablespoon fresh lime juice
- 1 teaspoon lime zest
- 1/2 teaspoon salt

1. **To make Pork:** In a medium bowl, whisk together avocado oil, coconut aminos, red chilli paste, mustard and erythritol. Set aside half of marinade. Add pork strips to bowl with remaining marinade and toss. Refrigerate pork covered for 30 minutes.
2. Preheat air fryer at 180°C for 3 minutes. Pour water in bottom of air fryer to ensure minimum smoke from fat drippings.
3. Add pork to ungreased air fryer basket. Cook for 7 minutes. Toss. Cook for an additional 10 minutes.
4. Transfer pork to bowl with remaining marinade and toss. Set aside.
5. **To make Cauliflower Rice:** In a large frying pan, heat coconut oil over medium-high heat for 30 seconds. Add riced cauliflower, spring onion whites and garlic. Toss, then place lid on frying pan, reduce heat to low, and let steam for 2 minutes.
6. Uncover frying pan and stir in coconut milk, lime juice, lime zest and salt. Let cook uncovered for an additional 5 minutes until heated through.
7. Serve pork over cauliflower rice and garnish with spring onion greens.

PER SERVING

KILOJOULES: 1414 | **FAT:** 24g | **PROTEIN:** 20g | **SODIUM:** 664mg | **FIBRE:** 2g | **CARBOHYDRATES:** 11g | **NET CARBOHYDRATES:** 7g | **SUGAR:** 4g

Texas Rib Eye Steak

The rib eye is a rugged cut of meat that takes on the barbecue sauce in this recipe like a boss. Savoury, spicy *and* salty, this dish is perfect served with a refreshing coleslaw or creamy cauliflower mash.

Hands-On Time: 10 minutes
Cook Time: 10 minutes

Serves 2

- **3/4 tablespoon water**
- **1/4 cup reduced sugar barbecue sauce**
- **1 clove garlic, peeled and minced**
- **1/8 teaspoon cayenne pepper**
- **1 (340 gram, 3cm-thick) rib eye steak**

1. Preheat air fryer at 200°C for 3 minutes. Pour water in bottom of air fryer to ensure minimum smoke from fat drippings.
2. Combine barbecue sauce, garlic and cayenne pepper in a small bowl. Divide in half. Slather steak with half of sauce.
3. Place steak in air fryer basket lightly greased with olive oil. Cook for 5 minutes. Flip steak. Brush with remaining sauce and cook for an additional 5 minutes or until cooked to your liking.
4. Transfer steak to a cutting board and let rest for 5 minutes, then slice and serve.

PER SERVING

KILOJOULES: 1113 | **FAT:** 12g | **PROTEIN:** 35g | **SODIUM:** 284mg | **FIBRE:** 0g | **CARBOHYDRATES:** 3g | **NET CARBOHYDRATES:** 3g | **SUGAR:** 11g

Bratwursts, Onions and Sauerkraut

If you would like to sub out the beef broth for beer when boiling the bratwurst, there are many low-carb beers available on the market. Just be sure to read labels, and enjoy a brew while the air fryer does its job!

Hands-On Time: 10 minutes
Cook Time: 21 minutes

Serves 4

- 450 grams uncooked pork bratwurst, each piece pierced with a fork twice
- 2 cups beef broth
- 2 cups water
- ½ medium brown onion, peeled and sliced into half-moons
- 2 cups drained sauerkraut
- 1½ tablespoons German mustard

1. Add bratwurst, beef broth, water and onion to a medium saucepan. Bring to a boil over high heat, then reduce heat to low and simmer 15 minutes. Drain.
2. Preheat air fryer at 200°C for 3 minutes.
3. Place bratwursts and onion in ungreased air fryer basket. Cook for 3 minutes. Flip bratwursts, add sauerkraut and cook for an additional 3 minutes. Using a meat thermometer, ensure internal temperature is at least 75°C.
4. Transfer bratwursts, onion and sauerkraut to a large serving plate and serve warm with mustard on the side.

PER SERVING

KILOJOULES: 1004 | **FAT:** 19g | **PROTEIN:** 11g | **SODIUM:** 1,537mg | **FIBRE:** 2g | **CARBOHYDRATES:** 7g | **NET CARBOHYDRATES:** 4g | **SUGAR:** 2g

Mushroom Swiss-Stuffed Pork Loins

Mushrooms and Swiss cheese are just one of those magical combinations. The pork loin is lean but still tender enough to lend some notes of rich fat to this tasty meal.

Hands-On Time: 10 minutes
Cook Time: 17 minutes

Serves 3

- 2 teaspoons olive oil
- ½ medium brown onion, peeled and diced
- ¾ cup diced white mushrooms
- ½ teaspoon salt
- ½ teaspoon freshly ground black pepper
- 3 (450 gram, approximately 3cm thick) boneless centre-cut pork loins, a pocket cut into each
- 6 thin slices Swiss cheese

1. In a medium frying pan, heat olive oil over medium-high heat for 2 minutes. Add onion and mushrooms and stir-fry for 3 minutes until onion is translucent. Add salt and pepper. Continue to cook for an additional minute.
2. Preheat air fryer at 180°C for 3 minutes.
3. Stuff an even amount of mushroom mixture into each pork chop pocket. Put 2 Swiss cheese slices into each pocket.
4. Place pork in air fryer basket lightly greased with olive oil. Cook for 11 minutes. Using a meat thermometer, ensure internal temperature is at least 70°C.
5. Transfer pork to a cutting board and let rest for 5 minutes before serving warm.

PER SERVING

KILOJOULES: 1782 | **FAT:** 31g | **PROTEIN:** 39g | **SODIUM:** 509mg | **FIBRE:** 1g | **CARBOHYDRATES:** 3g | **NET CARBOHYDRATES:** 2g | **SUGAR:** 1g

Orange Ginger Pork Lettuce Wraps

This sweet and spicy pork is a perfect complement to healthy, low-carb lettuce wraps. If you have leftovers, try serving them over a bed of riced cauliflower or even atop a mixed green salad.

Hands-On Time: 15 minutes
Cook Time: 20 minutes

Serves 4

- $^3/_4$ tablespoon arrowroot flour
- $^3/_4$ tablespoon water
- $^3/_4$ tablespoon apple cider vinegar
- 1 $^1/_2$ tablespoons sugar-reduced orange marmalade
- 1 teaspoon pulp-free orange juice
- 2 teaspoons sesame oil
- $^1/_8$ teaspoon cayenne pepper
- $^1/_4$ teaspoon ground ginger
- 1 (450 gram) boneless pork loin, cut into 3cm cubes
- $^1/_2$ teaspoon salt
- $^1/_4$ teaspoon freshly ground white pepper
- 8 iceberg lettuce leaves

WHAT IS A SLURRY?

A slurry is a starchy liquid used to thicken sauces, gravies or soups. It's usually made with cornstarch, flour, potato starch or arrowroot. Once mixed with water the slurry can be added directly to the hot liquid and bought to a simmer to thicken.

1. In a small bowl, create a slurry by whisking together arrowroot flour and water. Set aside.
2. In a small saucepan, combine apple cider vinegar, orange marmalade, orange juice, sesame oil, cayenne pepper and ginger over medium heat. Cook for 3 minutes, stirring continuously. Whisk in arrowroot slurry and heat for another minute. Remove pan from heat and allow to thicken for 3 minutes.
3. Preheat air fryer at 180°C for 3 minutes.
4. Season pork with salt and white pepper.
5. Add half of pork to air fryer basket lightly greased with olive oil. Cook for 4 minutes. Shake gently. Cook for an additional 4 minutes. Using a meat thermometer, ensure internal temperature is at least 62°C.
6. Transfer cooked pork to sauce. Repeat cooking with remaining pork, then add to sauce and toss. Serve warm in lettuce leaves.

PER SERVING

KILOJOULES: 1079 | **FAT:** 14g | **PROTEIN:** 22g | **SODIUM:** 335mg | **FIBRE:** 2g | **CARBOHYDRATES:** 11g | **NET CARBOHYDRATES:** 3g | **SUGAR:** 2g

Banh Mi-Inspired Pork Bowl

A typical banh mi is a baguette sandwich filled with a Vietnamese-seasoned meat and pickled vegetables. This salad mimics those flavours, making it an addictive (and low-carb) bowl that you'll want to make over and over again!

Hands-On Time: 10 minutes
Cook Time: 19 minutes

Serves 4

For Crema

- 3 tablespoons sour cream
- 3 tablespoons mayonnaise
- 3/4 tablespoon fresh lime juice
- 1/2 teaspoon salt

For Vegetables

- 4 medium radishes, julienned
- 1 medium shallot, peeled and thinly sliced
- 2 1/4 tablespoons apple cider vinegar
- 1/8 teaspoon salt
- 2 medium carrots, peeled and shaved into ribbons
- 4 cups shredded wombok cabbage
- 1/4 cup chopped fresh basil
- 1/4 cup chopped fresh mint

For Pork

- 3/4 tablespoon sesame oil
- 3/4 tablespoon coconut aminos
- 2 teaspoons red chilli paste
- 2 teaspoons erythritol sweetener
- 1 (3cm) knob fresh ginger, peeled and minced
- 1 (450 gram) pork shoulder, trimmed and thinly sliced into 3cm strips
- 1 1/2 tablespoons water

1. **To make Crema:** In a small bowl, whisk together ingredients. Refrigerate covered until ready to use.
2. **To make Vegetables:** In a medium bowl, add radishes, shallot, apple cider vinegar and salt. Refrigerate covered until ready to use.
3. **To make Pork:** In a medium bowl, whisk together sesame oil, coconut aminos, red chilli paste, erythritol and ginger. Set aside half of marinade. Add pork strips to bowl with remaining marinade and toss. Refrigerate covered until ready to use.
4. Preheat air fryer at 180°C for 3 minutes. Pour water in bottom of air fryer to ensure minimum smoke from fat drippings.
5. Add pork to ungreased air fryer basket. Cook for 5 minutes. Toss. Cook for 6 minutes. Toss once more and cook for an additional 6 minutes.
6. Transfer pork to bowl with remaining marinade and toss.
7. Add carrots to ungreased air fryer basket and cook for 2 minutes.
8. **To assemble:** Distribute cabbage, basil and mint in four medium bowls. Top with pork and vegetables. Drizzle crema over the top and serve.

PER SERVING

KILOJOULES: 1602 | **FAT:** 29g | **PROTEIN:** 20g | **SODIUM:** 740mg | **FIBRE:** 2g | **CARBOHYDRATES:** 12g | **NET CARBOHYDRATES:** 8g | **SUGAR:** 5g

Juicy Pork Meatballs

Eat these meatballs right out of the air fryer, tossed in some warmed no-sugar-added napolitana sauce or over a bed of steamed greens. The onion, yoghurt and cheese add a moistness that plays so nicely with the natural, juicy fattiness of ground pork. The almond flour and egg also help bind these meatballs together — you'll never miss the carb-filled bread crumbs!

Hands-On Time: 15 minutes
Cook Time: 16 minutes

Serves 4

- **450 grams pork mince**
- **1 large egg**
- **3/4 tablespoon plain Greek yoghurt**
- **1/4 cup peeled and grated brown onion**
- **1/4 cup finely chopped fresh parsley**
- **1/4 cup grated Parmesan cheese**
- **1 1/2 tablespoons almond flour**
- **1/4 teaspoon garlic powder**
- **1/4 teaspoon salt**
- **1/4 teaspoon freshly ground black pepper**

1. Preheat air fryer at 180°C for 3 minutes.
2. Combine all ingredients in a large bowl. Form into 16 meatballs.
3. Add eight meatballs to air fryer basket lightly greased with olive oil and cook for 6 minutes. Flip and cook for an additional 2 minutes.
4. Transfer cooked meatballs to a large serving plate. Repeat cooking with remaining meatballs. Serve warm.

PER SERVING

KILOJOULES: 1288 | **FAT:** 21g | **PROTEIN:** 26g | **SODIUM:** 312mg | **FIBRE:** 1g | **CARBOHYDRATES:** 3g | **NET CARBOHYDRATES:** 2g | **SUGAR:** 1g

Buffalo-Style Pork Meatballs

Whatever the occasion, these low-carb buffalo-style meatballs will be at the top of everyone's list. Choose the heat via the sauce that you purchase, and don't forget to read those labels for any hidden ingredients!

Hands-On Time: 15 minutes
Cook Time: 16 minutes

Serves 4

450 grams pork mince
1 large egg
¼ cup buffalo wing sauce
¼ cup grated celery
¼ cup finely chopped fresh parsley
¼ cup almond flour
¼ teaspoon salt

1. Preheat air fryer at 180°C for 3 minutes.
2. Combine all ingredients in a large bowl. Form into 16 meatballs.
3. Add eight meatballs to air fryer basket lightly greased with olive oil and cook 6 minutes. Flip and cook an additional 2 minutes.
4. Transfer cooked meatballs to a large serving plate. Repeat cooking with remaining meatballs. Serve warm.

PER SERVING

CALORIES: 303 | **FAT:** 22g | **PROTEIN:** 24g | **SODIUM:** 583mg | **FIBRE:** 1g | **CARBOHYDRATES:** 2g | **NET CARBOHYDRATES:** 1g | **SUGAR:** 1g

HOMEMADE BLUE CHEESE DRESSING

So simple, so fresh! Combine the following ingredients for some homemade blue cheese dressing: ½ cup mayonnaise, ¼ cup sour cream, 2 teaspoons full-cream milk or cream, 1 teaspoon lemon juice, 1 peeled and minced clove garlic, ¼ teaspoon salt, ¼ teaspoon freshly ground black pepper, ⅓ cup blue cheese crumbled and 1½ tablespoons chopped fresh chives. Cover with a lid and refrigerate for up to five days.

7

Fish and Seafood Main Dishes

Seafood is one of those meals that you may order a lot at restaurants but overlook at home. A terrific source of protein and other nutrients — not to mention low in carbs *and* calories — it is a fare worth embracing in your kitchen. A lot of home chefs are timid when it comes to cooking fish and shellfish, but it's time to conquer those fears — they make some of the quickest meals you can cook in your air fryer! The air fryer yields a crisp topping on a juicy fillet. In addition, your fried oyster, shrimp, fish finger and even calamari favourites can be enjoyed without the fatty cooking oil and carbs in traditional deep-fried foods.

From Crab-Stuffed Mushrooms to Smoky Fried Calamari and Tuna Croquettes, this chapter covers a variety of delicious fish and shellfish recipes that will have you eating seafood on a regular basis.

Oysters Rockefeller

Fresh oysters can be found in the fresh seafood section of most supermarkets. If you are not game to shuck the oysters yourself, ask your fishmonger. This is generally a task that they will provide at no additional cost. Tell them to save the shells, though, so you can make this delicious dish!

Hands-On Time: 10 minutes
Cook Time: 16 minutes

Serves 2

- **1 ½ tablespoons butter**
- **1 medium shallot, peeled and minced**
- **1 clove garlic, peeled and minced**
- **1 cup chopped fresh baby spinach**
- **4 teaspoons grated Parmesan cheese**
- **⅛ teaspoon Tabasco original hot sauce**
- **½ teaspoon fresh lemon juice**
- **¼ cup crushed garlic pork rinds**
- **12 oysters, on the half shell, rinsed and patted dry**

1. In a small frying pan, heat butter over medium heat for 30 seconds. Add shallot, garlic and spinach. Stir-fry for 3 minutes until shallot is translucent.
2. Add Parmesan cheese, Tabasco sauce, lemon juice and pork rinds to frying pan. Distribute mixture to tops of oysters.
3. Preheat air fryer at 200°C for 3 minutes.
4. Place half of oysters in ungreased air fryer basket. Cook for 6 minutes.
5. Transfer cooked oysters to a large serving plate and repeat cooking with remaining oysters. Serve warm.

PER SERVING

KILOJOULES: 828 | **FAT:** 15g | **PROTEIN:** 9g | **SODIUM:** 213mg | **FIBRE:** 1g | **CARBOHYDRATES:** 6g | **NET CARBOHYDRATES:** 5g | **SUGAR:** 2g

Steamer Clams

Littleneck clams are not only inexpensive, but they are also a lean source of protein with few carbs. Eat them alone or with some zoodles (zucchini noodles).

Hands-On Time: 20 minutes
Cook Time: 7 minutes

Serves 2

25 littleneck clams, scrubbed
1 1/2 tablespoons water
1 1/2 tablespoons butter, melted
2 lemon wedges

1. Place clams in a large bowl filled with water. Let stand for 10 minutes. Drain. Refill bowl with water and let stand for an additional 10 minutes. Drain.
2. Preheat air fryer at 180°C for 3 minutes.
3. Pour 2 tablespoons water into bottom of air fryer. Add clams to ungreased air fryer basket. Cook for 7 minutes. Discard any clams that don't open.
4. Remove clams from shells and add to a large serving dish with melted butter. Squeeze lemon on top and serve.

PER SERVING

KILOJOULES: 1167 | **FAT:** 14g | **PROTEIN:** 30g | **SODIUM:** 1,429mg | **FIBRE:** 0g | **CARBOHYDRATES:** 7g | **NET CARBOHYDRATES:** 7g | **SUGAR:** 0g

Seared Sea Scallops

The convection oven-style of cooking in the air fryer sears these scallops beautifully on all sides. Serve the scallops with steamed asparagus, mashed potatoes and a drizzle of fresh hollandaise sauce over everything for decadent bites of yummy!

Hands-On Time: 5 minutes
Cook Time: 8 minutes

Serves 2

1 1/2 tablespoons butter, melted
3/4 tablespoon fresh lemon juice
450 grams (about 10) jumbo sea scallops

1. Preheat air fryer at 200°C for 3 minutes.
2. In a small bowl, combine butter and lemon juice. Roll scallops in mixture to coat all sides.
3. Place scallops in ungreased air fryer basket. Cook for 2 minutes. Toss scallops. Cook for an additional 3 minutes. Serve warm.

PER SERVING

KILOJOULES: 1087 | **FAT:** 13g | **PROTEIN:** 27g | **SODIUM:** 891mg | **FIBRE:** 0g | **CARBOHYDRATES:** 8g | **NET CARBOHYDRATES:** 8g | **SUGAR:** 0g

Smoky Fried Calamari

Calamari can be found in the frozen section, sometimes already cut into circles; however, fresh squid tubes can be purchased at the fish counter, and they are easy to slice at home.

Hands-On Time: 15 minutes
Cook Time: 8 minutes

Serves 4

- **1 ½ tablespoons no-sugar-added tomato paste**
- **¾ tablespoon gochujang**
- **¾ tablespoon fresh lime juice**
- **1 teaspoon smoked paprika**
- **½ teaspoon salt**
- **1 cup crushed pork rinds**
- **150 grams (about 6) calamari tubes, cut into 6mm rings**

1. Preheat air fryer at 200°C for 3 minutes.
2. In a medium bowl, whisk together tomato paste, gochujang, lime juice, paprika and salt. Add pork rinds to a separate shallow dish.
3. Coat a calamari ring in tomato mixture. Shake off excess. Roll through pork rind crumbs. Repeat with remaining rings.
4. Place half of calamari rings in air fryer basket lightly greased with olive oil. Cook for 2 minutes. Gently flip and cook for an additional 2 minutes.
5. Transfer cooked calamari to a large serving dish and repeat cooking with remaining calamari. Serve warm.

PER SERVING

KILOJOULES: 414 | **FAT:** 3g | **PROTEIN:** 11g | **SODIUM:** 545mg | **FIBRE:** 1g | **CARBOHYDRATES:** 6g | **NET CARBOHYDRATES:** 5g | **SUGAR:** 2g

Battered Fish Fingers with Tartar Sauce

Cook these low-carb fish fingers for your kids or just for yourself to bring back some childhood memories. Cod is used in this recipe, but any firm whitefish works. You can even get experimental and try your hand at salmon ones!

Hands-On Time: 10 minutes
Cook Time: 20 minutes

Serves 4

For Tartar Sauce
- **1/2 cup mayonnaise**
- **3/4 tablespoon Dijon mustard**
- **1/2 cup small-diced dill pickles**
- **1/8 teaspoon salt**
- **1/4 teaspoon freshly ground black pepper**

For Fish Fingers
- **1 large egg, beaten**
- **1/4 cup arrowroot flour**
- **1/4 cup almond flour**
- **1/2 teaspoon salt**
- **1/4 teaspoon freshly ground black pepper**
- **450 grams cod, cut into 3cm fingers**

1. **To make Tartar Sauce:** Combine all ingredients in a small bowl and refrigerate covered until ready to use.
2. **To make Fish Fingers:** Preheat air fryer at 180°C for 3 minutes.
3. Place egg in a small bowl. Combine arrowroot flour, almond flour, salt and pepper in a separate shallow dish.
4. Dip a fish finger in egg. Shake off excess egg. Roll in flour mixture. Transfer to a large plate. Repeat with remaining fish fingers.
5. Place half of fish fingers in air fryer basket lightly greased with olive oil. Cook for 5 minutes. Carefully flip fish fingers. Cook for an additional 5 minutes.
6. Transfer cooked fish fingers to a large serving plate and repeat cooking with remaining fish fingers. Serve warm with tartar sauce on the side.

PER SERVING

KILOJOULES: 1518 | **FAT:** 26g | **PROTEIN:** 21g | **SODIUM:** 855mg | **FIBRE:** 1g | **CARBOHYDRATES:** 9g | **NET CARBOHYDRATES:** 8g | **SUGAR:** 1g

Crab Cakes with Rocket and Blackberry Salad

This is a simple yet elegant lunch filled with nutrients and flavour. You'll never know that the traditional carb-filled bread crumbs aren't in these crab cakes, as the sweet taste of the crab will shine through.

Hands-On Time: 15 minutes
Cook Time: 10 minutes

Serves 2

For Crab Cakes

- 230 grams lump crabmeat, shells discarded
- 1 1/2 tablespoons mayonnaise
- 1/2 teaspoon Dijon mustard
- 1/2 teaspoon lemon juice
- 2 teaspoons peeled and minced brown onion
- 1/4 teaspoon prepared horseradish
- 1/4 cup almond meal
- 1 large egg white, beaten
- 1/2 teaspoon Old Bay Seasoning

For Salad

- 3/4 tablespoon olive oil
- 2 teaspoons lemon juice
- 1/8 teaspoon salt
- 1/8 teaspoon freshly ground black pepper
- 110 grams fresh rocket
- 1/2 cup fresh blackberries
- 1/4 cup walnut pieces
- 2 lemon wedges

1. **To make Crab Cakes:** Preheat air fryer at 200°C for 3 minutes.
2. In a medium bowl, combine all ingredients. Form into four patties.
3. Place patties into air fryer basket lightly greased with olive oil. Cook for 5 minutes. Flip patties. Cook for an additional 5 minutes.
4. Transfer crab cakes to a large plate. Set aside.
5. **To make Salad:** In a large bowl, whisk together olive oil, lemon juice, salt and pepper. Add rocket and toss. Distribute into two medium bowls.
6. Add two crab cakes to each bowl. Garnish with blackberries, walnuts and lemon wedges. Serve.

PER SERVING

KILOJOULES: 1698 | **FAT:** 29g | **PROTEIN:** 29g | **SODIUM:** 790mg | **FIBRE:** 4g | **CARBOHYDRATES:** 10g | **NET CARBOHYDRATES:** 6g | **SUGAR:** 4g

Bacon-Wrapped Stuffed Prawns

Prawns stuffed with cheese and wrapped in bacon is an irresistible combination. Make sure you buy the large prawns for this recipe. The bacon takes longer to cook than small prawns, so the end result is better with a larger prawn.

Hands-On Time: 10 minutes
Cook Time: 18 minutes

Serves 4

- **450 grams (about 20) large raw prawns, deveined and shelled**
- **2 1/4 tablespoons crumbled goat cheese**
- **1 1/2 tablespoons panko bread crumbs**
- **1/4 teaspoon Worcestershire sauce**
- **1/2 teaspoon prepared horseradish**
- **1/4 teaspoon garlic powder**
- **2 teaspoons mayonnaise**
- **1/4 teaspoon freshly ground black pepper**
- **1 1/2 tablespoons water**
- **5 slices bacon, quartered**
- **1/4 cup chopped fresh parsley**

1. Butterfly prawns by cutting down the spine of each prawn without going all the way through.
2. In a medium bowl, combine goat cheese, bread crumbs, Worcestershire sauce, horseradish, garlic powder, mayonnaise and pepper.
3. Preheat air fryer at 200°C for 3 minutes. Pour 2 tablespoons water into bottom of air fryer.
4. Evenly press goat cheese mixture into prawns. Wrap a piece of bacon around each piece of prawn to hold in cheese mixture.
5. Place half of the prawns in fryer basket. Cook for 5 minutes. Flip prawns. Cook for an additional 4 minutes. Transfer to serving plate. Repeat with remaining prawns.
6. Garnish with chopped parsley. Serve warm.

PER SERVING

KILOJOULES: 728 | **FAT:** 8g | **PROTEIN:** 20g | **SODIUM:** 833mg | **FIBRE:** 0g | **CARBOHYDRATES:** 4g | **NET CARBOHYDRATES:** 3g | **SUGAR:** 0g

Simply Prawns

Prawns are not only high in protein, but they are also delicious and low in calories. Eat them plain, in a salad, warm, chilled or dipped! They are such a versatile and fairly inexpensive protein, and they can be made in a snap using your air fryer.

Hands-On Time: 5 minutes
Cook Time: 6 minutes

Serves 2

- **450 grams medium raw prawns, tail on, deveined, thawed or fresh**
- **1 ½ tablespoons butter, melted**
- **¾ tablespoon fresh lemon juice (about ½ medium lemon)**

1. Preheat air fryer at 180°C for 3 minutes.
2. In a large bowl, toss prawns in butter.
3. Place prawns in air fryer basket lightly greased with olive oil. Cook for 4 minutes. Gently flip prawns. Cook for an additional 2 minutes.
4. Transfer prawns to a large serving plate. Squeeze lemon juice over prawns and serve.

PER SERVING

KILOJOULES: 1108 | **FAT:** 14g | **PROTEIN:** 31g | **SODIUM:** 1,285mg | **FIBRE:** 0g | **CARBOHYDRATES:** 3g | **NET CARBOHYDRATES:** 3g | **SUGAR:** 0g

Chili Lime-Crusted Coral Trout

Pork rinds are such a great way to get in a little crunch without any of the carb-filled grain. Bread this trout with different flavours of pork rinds for more variety.

Hands-On Time: 10 minutes
Cook Time: 10 minutes

Serves 2

- **1 ½ tablespoons butter, melted**
- **½ cup crushed chilli lime-flavored pork rinds**
- **2 (170 gram) coral trout fillets**

1. Preheat air fryer at 180°F for 3 minutes.
2. Combine butter and pork rinds in a small bowl. Press mixture onto tops of trout fillets.
3. Place fish in air fryer basket lightly greased with olive oil. Cook for 10 minutes until fish is opaque and flakes easily with a fork.
4. Transfer fish to two medium plates and serve warm.

PER SERVING

KILOJOULES: 1125 | **FAT:** 15g | **PROTEIN:** 32g | **SODIUM:** 239mg | **FIBRE:** 0g | **CARBOHYDRATES:** 0g | **NET CARBOHYDRATES:** 0g | **SUGAR:** 0g

Tuna Croquettes

Traditionally, croquettes are a fried delicacy; the word *croquette* comes from the French word *croquer*, which literally means "crunch." With the air fryer, however, you'll get all the crispness without the deep-fried fat and carbs. Also, don't discard your celery leaves — chop them up and serve them over your croquettes, or add them to a salad at a later date!

Hands-On Time: 15 minutes
Cook Time: 24 minutes

Serves 4

- **340 grams canned tuna in water, drained**
- **1/3 cup mayonnaise**
- **3/4 tablespoon minced fresh celery**
- **2 teaspoons dried dill, divided**
- **1 teaspoon fresh lime juice**
- **1 cup crushed pork rinds, divided**
- **1 large egg**
- **1 teaspoon prepared horseradish**

1. Preheat air fryer at 190°C for 3 minutes.
2. In a medium bowl, combine tuna, mayonnaise, celery, 1 teaspoon dill, lime juice, 1/4 cup pork rinds, egg and horseradish.
3. Form mixture into 12 rectangular mound shapes (about 2 tablespoons each). Roll each croquette in a shallow dish with remaining crushed pork rinds.
4. Place six croquettes in air fryer basket lightly greased with olive oil. Cook for 4 minutes. Gently turn one third. Cook for an additional 4 minutes. Gently turn another third. Cook for an additional 4 minutes.
5. Transfer cooked croquettes to a large serving dish. Repeat cooking with remaining croquettes and garnish with remaining dill. Serve warm.

PER SERVING

KILOJOULES: 1008 | **FAT:** 18g | **PROTEIN:** 19g | **SODIUM:** 440mg | **FIBRE:** 0g | **CARBOHYDRATES:** 0g | **NET CARBOHYDRATES:** 0g | **SUGAR:** 0g

Buttery Lobster Tails

Whether you are cooking them to eat as a main course, chopped into a lettuce wrap or sliced atop a salad, these buttery lobster tails are a luxurious low-carb, low-kilojoule protein that is sure to please!

Hands-On Time: 10 minutes
Cook Time: 8 minutes

Serves 2

- **2 (170 gram) uncooked lobster tails, thawed**
- **¾ tablespoon butter, melted**
- **½ teaspoon Old Bay Seasoning**
- **½ tablespoon chopped fresh parsley**
- **2 lemon wedges**

MAKING BROTH WITH LOBSTER TAIL SHELLS

Don't discard those empty lobster tail shells, as they can be used for a beautiful broth for lobster bisque, crab soup or seafood gumbo. Place the shells in a Dutch oven or heavy-bottomed pot with 4 cups water, 1 medium peeled and diced yellow onion, 1 medium peeled and diced carrot, 1 diced stalk celery, and 2 peeled and halved cloves garlic. Bring to a boil over high heat. Reduce heat and simmer covered for 30 minutes. Use a slotted spoon to remove and discard the solids from the broth. Strain the remaining liquid through a fine-mesh sieve or cheesecloth. Refrigerate covered for up to four days or freeze up to six months.

1. Preheat air fryer at 200°C for 3 minutes.
2. Using kitchen shears, cut down the middle of each lobster tail on the softer side. Carefully run your finger between the lobster meat and the shell to loosen meat.
3. Place lobster tails in ungreased air fryer basket, cut sides up. Cook for 4 minutes. Brush with butter and sprinkle with Old Bay Seasoning. Cook for an additional 4 minutes.
4. Serve warm, garnished with parsley and lemon wedges.

PER SERVING

CALORIES: 154 | **FAT:** 7g | **PROTEIN:** 21g | **SODIUM:** 889mg | **FIBRE:** 0g | **CARBOHYDRATES:** 1g | **NET CARBOHYDRATES:** 1g | **SUGAR:** 0g

Tuna Melts on Tomatoes

Put aside those carb-filled English muffins, tuna salad doesn't need them anymore! Choose ripe red tomatoes for slices that will be the base for this tasty meal.

Hands-On Time: 10 minutes
Cook Time: 4 minutes

Serves 2

- 170 grams canned tuna in water, drained
- 1/4 cup mayonnaise
- 2 teaspoons yellow mustard
- 1 tablespoon dill pickle, finely chopped
- 3/4 tablespoon celery, finely chopped
- 3/4 tablespoon peeled and finely chopped brown onion
- 1/8 teaspoon salt
- 1/8 teaspoon freshly ground black pepper
- 4 thick slices of a large tomato
- 1 small avocado, peeled, pitted and cut into 8 slices
- 1/2 cup grated mild Cheddar cheese

1. Combine tuna, mayonnaise, mustard, pickles, celery, onion, salt and pepper in a medium bowl.
2. Preheat air fryer at 180°C for 3 minutes.
3. Cut a piece of baking paper to fit the bottom of the air fryer basket. Place tomato slices on paper in single layer. Place two avocado slices on each tomato slice. Distribute tuna salad over avocado slices. Top evenly with cheese.
4. Place stacks in ungreased air fryer basket and cook for 4 minutes until cheese starts to brown. Serve warm.

PER SERVING

KILOJOULES: 2225 | **FAT:** 46g | **PROTEIN:** 22g | **SODIUM:** 762mg | **FIBRE:** 8g | **CARBOHYDRATES:** 13g | **NET CARBOHYDRATES:** 5g | **SUGAR:** 3g

Classic Lobster Salad

This luscious salad pairs perfectly with a glass of dry white wine or chilled rosé. The tarragon can be switched out for dill, and if you have only a lime on hand, use it instead of the lemon. Always remember that you can tailor recipes to your taste buds (or the ingredients in your refrigerator). Have fun and make it your own recipe!

Hands-On Time: 10 minutes
Cook Time: 8 minutes

Serves 2

- 2 (170 gram) uncooked lobster tails
- 1/4 cup mayonnaise
- 2 teaspoons fresh lemon juice
- 1 small stalk celery, sliced
- 2 teaspoons chopped fresh chives
- 2 teaspoons chopped fresh tarragon
- 1/4 teaspoon salt
- 1/8 teaspoon freshly ground black pepper
- 2 thick slices of a large tomato
- 1 small avocado, peeled, pitted and diced

1. Preheat air fryer at 200°C for 3 minutes.
2. Using kitchen shears, cut down the middle of each lobster tail on the softer side. Carefully run your finger between the lobster meat and the shell to loosen meat.
3. Place lobster tails, cut sides up, in ungreased air fryer basket. Cook for 8 minutes.
4. Transfer tails to a large plate and let cool for about 3 minutes until easy to handle, then pull lobster meat from shell. Roughly chop meat and add to a medium bowl.
5. Add mayonnaise, lemon juice, celery, chives, tarragon, salt and pepper to bowl. Combine.
6. Divide lobster salad between two medium plates, top with tomato slices and garnish with avocado. Serve.

PER SERVING

KILOJOULES: 1937 | **FAT:** 36g | **PROTEIN:** 24g | **SODIUM:** 1,343mg | **FIBRE:** 7g | **CARBOHYDRATES:** 12g | **NET CARBOHYDRATES:** 5g | **SUGAR:** 3g

Baked Avocados with Smoked Salmon

This meal is exploding with flavours and nutrients. Air frying avocados not only heats them up but also softens the flesh. The caper and cream cheese mixture also lends a smooth and salty topping that pairs well with the salmon. You won't believe it's low-carb!

Hands-On Time: 10 minutes
Cook Time: 8 minutes

Serves 2

- **¼ cup apple cider vinegar**
- **1 teaspoon erythritol sweetener**
- **¼ cup peeled and sliced red onion**
- **56 grams cream cheese, room temperature**
- **¾ tablespoon capers, drained**
- **2 large avocados, peeled, halved and pitted**
- **110 grams smoked salmon**
- **2 medium cherry tomatoes, halved**

1. In a small saucepan, heat apple cider vinegar and erythritol over high heat for 4 minutes until boiling. Add onion and remove saucepan from heat. Let set while preparing remaining ingredients. Drain when ready to use onions.
2. Combine cream cheese and capers in a small bowl. Cover and refrigerate until ready to use.
3. Preheat air fryer at 180°C for 3 minutes.
4. Place avocado halves, cut sides up, in ungreased air fryer basket and cook for 4 minutes.
5. Transfer avocados to two medium plates and garnish with cream cheese mixture, smoked salmon, pickled onions and tomato halves. Serve.

PER SERVING

KILOJOULES: 2096 | **FAT:** 42g | **PROTEIN:** 16g | **SODIUM:** 590mg | **FIBRE:** 14g | **CARBOHYDRATES:** 22g | **NET CARBOHYDRATES:** 6g | **SUGAR:** 3g

Salmon Cakes with Lemon Caper Sauce

This recipe calls for canned salmon for ease; however, leftover or freshly cooked salmon flaked into pieces are both great options for these powerhouse patties with omega-3 fatty acids.

Hands-On Time: 10 minutes
Cook Time: 20 minutes

Serves 4

For Lemon Caper Sauce
- 1/4 cup sour cream
- 1 1/2 tablespoons mayonnaise
- 2 cloves garlic, peeled and minced
- 1/4 teaspoon caper juice
- 2 teaspoons lemon juice

For Salmon Patties
- 1 (425 gram) can salmon, drained
- 1/2 cup mayonnaise
- 2 teaspoons lemon zest
- 1 large egg
- 1 1/2 tablespoons seeded and finely chopped red capsicum
- 1/2 cup almond meal
- 1/8 teaspoon salt
- 1 1/2 tablespoons capers, drained

1. **To make Lemon Caper Sauce:** In a small bowl, combine sour cream, mayonnaise, garlic, caper juice and lemon juice. Refrigerate covered until ready to use.
2. **To make Salmon Patties:** Preheat air fryer at 200°C for 3 minutes.
3. In a medium bowl, combine salmon, mayonnaise, lemon zest, egg, capsicum, almond meal and salt. Form into eight patties.
4. Place four patties in air fryer basket lightly greased with olive oil. Cook for 5 minutes. Gently flip and cook for an additional 5 minutes.
5. Transfer cooked patties to a large serving dish and repeat cooking with remaining patties. Let rest for 5 minutes, then drizzle with lemon caper sauce and garnish with capers. Serve.

PER SERVING

KILOJOULES: 1970 | **FAT:** 41g | **PROTEIN:** 21g | **SODIUM:** 832mg | **FIBRE:** 2g | **CARBOHYDRATES:** 5g | **NET CARBOHYDRATES:** 3g | **SUGAR:** 1g

Crab-Stuffed Mushrooms

As a full meal, side dish or appetiser, these scrumptious and creamy crab-stuffed mushrooms have a nice crunch from the bread crumb topping made crisp in the air fryer.

Hands-On Time: 10 minutes
Cook Time: 20 minutes

Serves 6

- 56 grams cream cheese, at room temperature
- 1/2 cup crabmeat, shells discarded
- 1 teaspoon prepared horseradish
- 1 teaspoon lemon juice
- 1/2 teaspoon salt
- 1/2 teaspoon freshly ground black pepper
- 450 grams brown mushrooms, stems removed
- 1 1/2 tablespoons panko bread crumbs
- 1 1/2 tablespoons butter, melted
- 1/4 cup chopped fresh parsley

1. In a medium bowl, combine cream cheese, crabmeat, horseradish, lemon juice, salt and pepper.
2. Preheat air fryer at 180°C for 5 minutes.
3. Evenly stuff cream cheese mixture into mushroom caps. Distribute bread crumbs over stuffed mushrooms. Drizzle melted butter over bread crumbs.
4. Place half of mushrooms in fryer basket. Cook for 10 minutes. Transfer to serving plate. Repeat with remaining mushrooms.
5. Garnish with chopped parsley. Serve warm.

PER SERVING

KILOJOULES: 414 | **FAT:** 7g | **PROTEIN:** 5g | **SODIUM:** 274mg | **FIBRE:** 1g | **CARBOHYDRATES:** 5g | **NET CARBOHYDRATES:** 4g | **SUGAR:** 2g

Dijon Pork Crusted Cod

The pork rinds lend a crunchiness and a "bready" quality — without the carbs. You can find pork rinds in a variety of flavours, so don't be afraid to experiment or to even make your own by crushing your own pork rinds.

Hands-On Time: 10 minutes
Cook Time: 10 minutes

Serves 2

1/2 cup crushed pork rinds
1/8 teaspoon salt
3/4 tablespoon Dijon mustard
1 teaspoon fresh lemon juice
1 tablespoon butter, melted
2 (170 gram) cod fillets

1. Preheat air fryer at 180°C for 3 minutes.
2. In a small bowl, combine pork rinds, salt, mustard, lemon juice and butter. Press mixture evenly across tops of cod fillets. Place cod in air fryer basket lightly greased with olive oil.
3. Cook cod for 10 minutes until opaque and flakes easily with a fork.
4. Transfer fillets to two medium plates and serve warm.

PER SERVING

KILOJOULES: 1112 | **FAT:** 9g | **PROTEIN:** 32g | **SODIUM:** 563mg | **FIBRE:** 0g | **CARBOHYDRATES:** 0g | **NET CARBOHYDRATES:** 0g | **SUGAR:** 0g

Fried Sardines with Romesco Dipping Sauce

Sardines can have a bad reputation, but seriously, they taste amazing and are packed with omega-3s, vitamin D, protein and selenium. And as a bonus, they are economical and low in mercury and other metals commonly found in fish. Paired with the low-carb romesco sauce, this is one delicious meal!

Hands-On Time: 5 minutes
Cook Time: 6 minutes

Serves 2

½ cup crushed pork rinds
2 (110 gram) cans skinless, boneless sardines packed in oil, drained
½ cup warmed romesco sauce

HOW TO MAKE A QUICK AND EASY ROMESCO SAUCE

Heat the following ingredients in a medium saucepan over medium-high heat for 5 minutes: 1 (340 gram) jar drained roasted capsicum, ½ cup canned drained diced tomatoes, ½ cup chopped fresh parsley, 2 peeled and halved cloves garlic, ½ cup chopped almonds, ¼ cup olive oil, ¾ tablespoon cooking sherry, ½ teaspoon smoked paprika, ¼ teaspoon cayenne pepper, ½ teaspoon salt and ¼ teaspoon freshly ground black pepper. Transfer to a blender and blend until smooth. Pour sauce into an airtight container and refrigerate for up to five days. Makes approximately 2 cups.

1. Preheat air fryer at 180°C for 3 minutes.
2. Place ground pork rinds in a shallow dish. Roll sardines to coat with ground pork rinds.
3. Place coated sardines in air fryer basket lightly greased with olive oil. Cook 3 minutes. Gently flip sardines and cook an additional 3 minutes.
4. Transfer to a medium serving dish and serve warm with romesco sauce.

PER SERVING

KILOJOULES: 1845 | **FAT:** 36g | **PROTEIN:** 23g | **SODIUM:** 836mg | **FIBRE:** 3g | **CARBOHYDRATES:** 4g | **NET CARBOHYDRATES:** 1g | **SUGAR:** 1g

Pesto Rainbow Trout Roulade

Rainbow trout is the perfect vessel for the fresh and bright flavours of pesto. Topping the roulade with crushed cornflakes adds a layer of texture, making these simple ingredients shine.

Hands-On Time: 15 minutes
Cook Time: 6 minutes

Serves 4

- 4 (140 gram) rainbow trout fillets
- 1 large egg
- 1 ½ tablespoons water
- 1 cup crushed cornflakes
- 1 teaspoon salt
- ½ teaspoon freshly ground black pepper
- 4 teaspoons pesto
- 1 ½ tablespoons butter, melted
- 4 lime wedges

1. Between two pieces of baking paper, gently pound fish fillets until "rollable", about 6mm thickness.
2. In a small bowl, whisk together egg and water.
3. In a shallow dish, combine cornflakes, salt and pepper.
4. Preheat air fryer at 180°C for 3 minutes.
5. Spread 1 teaspoon pesto on each fish fillet. Tightly and gently roll a fillet from one short end to the other. Secure with a toothpick. Repeat with each fillet.
6. Roll each fillet in egg mixture and coat in cornflake mixture.
7. Place fish in lightly greased air fryer basket. Drizzle tops with melted butter. Cook for 6 minutes.
8. Transfer to a serving dish and let rest for 5 minutes. Remove toothpicks. Serve warm with lime wedges.

PER SERVING

KILOJOULES: 724 | **FAT:** 10g | **PROTEIN:** 16g | **SODIUM:** 576mg | **FIBRE:** 1g | **CARBOHYDRATES:** 5g | **NET CARBOHYDRATES:** 5g | **SUGAR:** 1g

Cajun Cod with Prawn Mango Salsa

The heat from the Cajun seasoning is tempered by the soothing mango, tomatoes and prawns in this decadent salsa.

Hands-On Time: 10 minutes
Cook Time: 10 minutes

Serves 2

For Prawn Mango Salsa

- 1/4 cup chopped cooked prawns (see Simply Prawns recipe on page 153)
- 1/4 cup peeled and diced mango
- 1 medium Roma tomato, cored, seeded and diced
- 1 1/2 tablespoons peeled and diced red onion
- 3/4 tablespoon chopped fresh parsley
- 2 teaspoons fresh lime juice
- 1/4 teaspoon salt
- 1/4 teaspoon freshly ground black pepper

For Cod

- 2 (170 gram) cod fillets
- 2 teaspoons Cajun seasoning

1. **To make Prawn Mango Salsa:** Combine all ingredients in a medium bowl. Refrigerate covered until ready to use.
2. **To make Cod:** Preheat air fryer at 350°F for 3 minutes.
3. Season cod with Cajun seasoning. Place fish in air fryer basket lightly greased with olive oil.
4. Cook cod for 10 minutes until opaque and flakes easily with a fork.
5. Transfer cod to two medium plates and serve warm topped with salsa.

PER SERVING

KILOJOULES: 800 | **FAT:** 3g | **PROTEIN:** 30g | **SODIUM:** 467mg | **FIBRE:** 1g | **CARBOHYDRATES:** 9g | **NET CARBOHYDRATES:** 8g | **SUGAR:** 5g

ALTERING THIS RECIPE

The cod can be subbed out for any flaky whitefish, such as coral trout, bass or barramundi. If you want a little more kick, add a pepper such as a jalapeño, diced, to your salsa. And, if you like corriander, switch out the parsley for some of this fresh herb!

Lemon Garlic Barramundi

Barramundi is a little meatier than most whitefish, its buttery nature has a melt-in-your mouth texture. Simply seasoned with lemon juice, a little garlic and some fresh parsley, this low-carb fish dish is one for the books.

Hands-On Time: 5 minutes
Cook Time: 7 minutes

Serves 2

- **3/4 tablespoon butter, melted**
- **2 cloves garlic, peeled and minced**
- **3/4 tablespoon fresh lemon juice**
- **1/4 teaspoon salt**
- **2 (170 gram, 3cm thick) barramundi fillets**
- **2 teaspoons chopped fresh parsley**

1. Preheat air fryer at 190°C for 3 minutes.
2. In a small bowl, combine butter, garlic, lemon juice and salt. Rub mixture over tops of fillets.
3. Place sea bass in ungreased air fryer basket. Cook for 7 minutes.
4. Transfer barramundi to two medium plates and let rest for 5 minutes, then garnish with chopped parsley. Serve warm.

PER SERVING

KILOJOULES: 928 | **FAT:** 9g | **PROTEIN:** 32g | **SODIUM:** 408mg | **FIBRE:** 0g | **CARBOHYDRATES:** 2g | **NET CARBOHYDRATES:** 1g | **SUGAR:** 0g

8

Vegetarian Dishes

When eating a low-carb diet, coupled with being a vegetarian, your meal options can feel that much slimmer — not to mention trying to ensure the foods you *do* eat are nutritious. Fortunately, the air fryer is here to help, providing countless choices for low-carb vegetarian recipes that still manage to save you time in the kitchen. Whether you are a full-time vegetarian or just interested in Meatless Mondays, the air fryer has got you covered.

And the low-carb vegetarian dishes in this chapter will help you hit the spot. With recipes like Mexican Topped Avocados, Vegetable-Stuffed Mushrooms and Creamy Pesto Spaghetti Squash, you're sure to find new favourites!

Mexican Topped Avocados

If you'd like to bump up the protein factor, add some beans on top of the avocado before distributing the cheese. Some beans are higher in carbs, but they are counterbalanced by the fibre and are accepted on low-carb diets in small amounts. Try a spoonful of lentils, black beans or pinto beans.

Hands-On Time: 10 minutes
Cook Time: 4 minutes

Serves 2

- 1 cup seeded and diced tomatoes
- 3/4 tablespoon fresh lime juice
- 1 teaspoon lime zest
- 1 1/2 tablespoons chopped fresh coriander
- 1 small jalapeño, seeded and finely chopped
- 2 cloves garlic, peeled and minced
- 3/4 tablespoon peeled and diced red onion
- 1/2 teaspoon salt
- 2 large avocados, halved and pitted
- 3 tablespoons vegan Cheddar

1. Combine tomatoes, lime juice, lime zest, coriander, jalapeño, garlic, onion and salt in a medium bowl. Cover and refrigerate until ready to use.
2. Preheat air fryer at 180°C for 3 minutes.
3. Place avocado halves, cut sides up, in ungreased air fryer. Distribute cheese to top of avocado halves. Cook for 4 minutes.
4. Transfer avocados to a large serving plate, garnish with tomato mixture and serve.

PER SERVING

KILOJOULES: 719 | **FAT:** 14g | **PROTEIN:** 2g | **SODIUM:** 349mg | **FIBRE:** 6g | **CARBOHYDRATES:** 12g | **NET CARBOHYDRATES:** 6g | **SUGAR:** 2g

Taco Tuesday Fried Avocado Lettuce Wraps

Who needs carb-filled tortillas when all of the flavour is in the filling? Top these wraps with a dollop of sour cream or add in a dash of hot sauce if you like things spicy.

Hands-On Time: 15 minutes
Cook Time: 10 minutes

Serves 4

For Spicy Mayonnaise

- 1/2 cup vegan mayonnaise
- 2 teaspoons gochujang
- 1 teaspoon fresh lime juice
- 1/8 teaspoon salt

For Salsa

- 2 medium Roma tomatoes, cored, seeded and diced
- 1/4 cup peeled and finely diced red onion
- 2 cloves garlic, peeled and minced
- 3/4 tablespoon fresh lime juice
- 1 teaspoon fresh lime zest
- 1/4 cup chopped fresh coriander
- 1 teaspoon salt

For Avocado Fries

- Egg substitute equaling 1 large egg (see note on page 172)
- 1 1/2 tablespoons unsweetened almond milk
- 1 cup almond flour
- 1/4 cup ground flaxseed
- 1 large avocado, peeled, halved, pitted and cut into 12 "fries"

For Lettuce Wraps

- 6 large leaves iceberg lettuce
- 1 cup coleslaw mix (shredded cabbage and carrot)

1. **To make Spicy Mayonnaise:** In a small bowl, combine all ingredients and refrigerate covered until ready to use.
2. **To make Salsa:** In a medium bowl, combine all ingredients and refrigerate covered until ready to use.
3. **To make Avocado Fries:** Preheat air fryer at 190° for 3 minutes.
4. Whisk together egg substitute and almond milk in a small bowl. Combine almond flour and flaxseed in a separate shallow dish.
5. Dip avocado fries in egg substitute mixture. Coat in almond flour mixture to coat.
6. Place half of avocado fries in ungreased air fryer basket. Cook for 5 minutes, then transfer to a large serving plate. Repeat cooking with remaining avocado fries.
7. **To make Lettuce Wraps:** Add two avocado fries to each lettuce wrap. Top with coleslaw mix, spicy mayonnaise and salsa. Serve immediately.

PER SERVING

KILOJOULES: 1765 | **FAT:** 37g | **PROTEIN:** 11g | **SODIUM:** 935mg | **FIBRE:** 11g | **CARBOHYDRATES:** 23g | **NET CARBOHYDRATES:** 12g | **SUGAR:** 6g

Jackfruit "Fish" Fritters

Jackfruit is neutral enough to take on the flavours that you add to it, while the nori and Cajun seasonings trick the taste buds into reminding you of fish flavours.

Hands-On Time: 10 minutes
Cook Time: 20 minutes

Serves 4

- 570 grams canned jackfruit, drained and chopped
- 1 flax egg (see note)
- 3/4 tablespoon Dijon mustard
- 3/4 tablespoon vegan mayonnaise
- 3/4 tablespoon prepared horseradish
- 1 1/2 tablespoons peeled and grated brown onion
- 1 1/2 tablespoons chopped fresh parsley
- 1 1/2 tablespoons chopped nori
- 1 1/2 tablespoons almond flour
- 3/4 tablespoon Cajun seasoning
- 1/4 teaspoon garlic powder
- 1/4 teaspoon salt
- 2 lemon wedges

1. Combine all ingredients except lemon wedges in a medium bowl. Refrigerate covered 15 minutes.
2. Preheat air fryer at 180°C for 3 minutes. Cut a piece of baking paper to fit bottom of air fryer basket.
3. Form chilled mixture into 12 balls, approximately 2 tablespoons each. Place six balls in ungreased air fryer basket. Cook for 10 minutes.
4. Transfer to a large plate and repeat cooking with remaining balls. Serve warm garnished with lemon wedges.

PER SERVING

KILOJOULES: 435 | **FAT:** 5g | **PROTEIN:** 1g | **SODIUM:** 413mg | **FIBRE:** 6g | **CARBOHYDRATES:** 11g | **NET CARBOHYDRATES:** 5g | **SUGAR:** 4g

WHAT IS A FLAX EGG?

There are many vegan and vegetarian egg substitutions on the market, but one that is easy to make in your kitchen is 1 1/2 tablespoons ground flaxseed combined with 4 1/2 tablespoons water. Let it set for about 15 minutes before using in a recipe. This combination equals one large egg.

Vegetable-Stuffed Mushrooms

Whether you are entertaining guests or just entertaining your own taste buds, this recipe is filled with low-carb "meaty" flavours that will satisfy the pickiest of folks.

Hands-On Time: 10 minutes
Cook Time: 5 minutes

Serves 2

3 teaspoons olive oil, divided
12 whole white button mushroom caps
1 ½ tablespoons diced white button mushroom stems
1 ½ tablespoons small-diced yellow squash
1 teaspoon nutritional yeast
¼ teaspoon salt
1 ½ tablespoons no-sugar-added tomato paste
¾ tablespoon chopped fresh parsley

1. Brush 1 teaspoon olive oil around top ridge of mushroom caps.
2. Preheat air fryer at 180°C for 3 minutes.
3. In a medium bowl, combine mushroom stems, squash, nutritional yeast, salt, remaining olive oil and tomato paste. Distribute and press mixture into tops of mushroom caps.
4. Place stuffed mushrooms in ungreased air fryer basket. Cook for 5 minutes.
5. Transfer mushrooms to a medium plate and garnish with parsley. Serve.

PER SERVING

KILOJOULES: 355 | **FAT:** 7g | **PROTEIN:** 2g | **SODIUM:** 305mg | **FIBRE:** 1g | **CARBOHYDRATES:** 5g | **NET CARBOHYDRATES:** 4g | **SUGAR:** 3g

Mushroom and Onion Pizza Rounds

Serve these low-carb pizza rounds alongside a fresh mixed green salad for a tummy full of healthy ingredients. If you don't eat dairy, substitute with vegan mozzarella which you can find at your local supermarket.

Hands-On Time: 10 minutes
Cook Time: 15 minutes

Serves 4

- **2 teaspoons plus 2 tablespoons olive oil, divided**
- **1/4 cup peeled and small-diced yellow onion**
- **1/2 cup small-diced baby Swiss brown mushrooms**
- **1/2 cup no-sugar-added napolitana sauce**
- **1 small eggplant, sliced into circles**
- **1 teaspoon salt**
- **1 cup shredded mozzarella**
- **1/4 cup chopped fresh basil**

1. In a medium frying pan, heat 2 teaspoons olive oil over medium heat for 30 seconds. Add onion and mushrooms. Cook for 4 minutes until onion is translucent. Add napolitana sauce and stir. Remove from heat.
2. Preheat air fryer at 190°C for 3 minutes.
3. Rub remaining 2 tablespoons olive oil over both sides of eggplant circles. Lay out slices on a large plate and season evenly with salt. Top evenly with sauce mixture and shredded mozzarella.
4. Place half of eggplant pizzas in ungreased air fryer basket. Cook for 5 minutes. Transfer back to plate. Repeat cooking with remaining pizzas.
5. Garnish pizzas with chopped basil and serve warm.

PER SERVING

KILOJOULES: 749 | **FAT:** 14g | **PROTEIN:** 8g | **SODIUM:** 816mg | **FIBRE:** 2g | **CARBOHYDRATES:** 6g | **NET CARBOHYDRATES:** 4g | **SUGAR:** 3g

Barbecue Jackfruit Lettuce Wraps with Coleslaw

Whether you like your barbecue sauce spicy or neutral, choose a sugar-free version to keep things low-carb. The jackfruit will take on its flavour, and the cool coleslaw will meld nicely with whatever sauce you choose.

Hands-On Time: 10 minutes
Cook Time: 10 minutes

Serves 3

For Coleslaw
- 1 cup prepackaged coleslaw mix
- 1/4 cup vegan mayonnaise
- 2 teaspoons erythritol sweetener
- 1/2 teaspoon apple cider vinegar
- 1/4 teaspoon salt
- 1/4 teaspoon freshly ground black pepper

For Jackfruit Wraps
- 570 grams canned green jackfruit in brine, drained and diced
- 2/3 cup reduced-sugar barbecue sauce, divided
- 6 large leaves iceberg lettuce

1. **To make Coleslaw:** In a medium bowl, combine all ingredients. Refrigerate covered until ready to use.
2. **To make Jackfruit Wraps:** Preheat air fryer at 190°C for 3 minutes.
3. Toss 1/3 cup barbecue sauce with jackfruit in a medium bowl.
4. Place jackfruit in air fryer basket lightly greased with olive oil and cook for 5 minutes. Shake basket. Cook for an additional 5 minutes.
5. Transfer jackfruit to a medium bowl. Add remaining sauce. Using two forks, pull apart jackfruit until it resembles pulled pork.
6. Serve jackfruit on lettuce leaves topped with coleslaw.

PER SERVING

KILOJOULES: 807 | **FAT:** 10g | **PROTEIN:** 1g | **SODIUM:** 895mg | **FIBRE:** 9g | **CARBOHYDRATES:** 22g | **NET CARBOHYDRATES:** 11g | **SUGAR:** 25g

WHAT IS JACKFRUIT?

Jackfruit is a highly nutritious fruit that can be found fresh or canned. Depending on the ripeness of the fruit, it can be used in sweet or savoury dishes. When not ripened, it has a neutral flavour that makes it an amazing meat replacement that will take on the flavour it is paired with.

Greek Eggplant Rounds

Eggplants are rich in fibre and antioxidants and they're a feature of the Mediterranean diet. Although any eggplant will work with this recipe, try selecting one that has a longer, slimmer shape as it will yield more consistent rounds when sliced.

Hands-On Time: 10 minutes
Cook Time: 10 minutes

Serves 4

- 2 teaspoons olive oil
- 1 long, narrow eggplant, sliced into rounds
- ½ teaspoon salt
- ½ cup no-sugar-added napolitana sauce
- ½ cup fetta cheese crumbles
- 8 Kalamata olives, pitted and halved
- 1 ½ tablespoons chopped fresh dill

1. Preheat air fryer at 180°C for 3 minutes.
2. Rub olive oil over both sides of eggplant circles. Lay out slices on a large plate and season evenly with salt. Top evenly with napolitana sauce, fetta crumbles and olives.
3. Place half of eggplant pizzas in ungreased air fryer basket. Cook for 5 minutes. Transfer back to plate. Repeat cooking with remaining pizzas.
4. Garnish with chopped dill and serve warm.

PER SERVING

KILOJOULES: 343 | **FAT:** 5g | **PROTEIN:** 2g | **SODIUM:** 387mg | **FIBRE:** 2g | **CARBOHYDRATES:** 7g | **NET CARBOHYDRATES:** 5g | **SUGAR:** 4g

Buddha Bowls

Packed with vegetables, riced cauliflower, rocket and pine nuts, these low-carb bowls are overflowing with flavour, texture and nutrition. The heartiness of the ingredients will ensure that you stay full and satisfied for many hours.

Hands-On Time: 5 minutes
Cook Time: 14 minutes

Serves 4

- 1 large carrot, peeled and julienned
- 1/4 cup apple cider vinegar
- 1/2 teaspoon ground ginger
- 1/8 teaspoon cayenne pepper
- 1/2 small brown onion, peeled and sliced into half-moons
- 1 medium parsnip, peeled and diced
- 1 teaspoon avocado oil
- 110 grams extra-firm tofu, drained and cut into 6mm cubes
- 1/2 teaspoon five-spice powder
- 1/2 teaspoon chilli powder
- 2 teaspoons fresh lime zest
- 1 cup fresh rocket
- 1/2 cup steamed riced cauliflower
- 1 small avocado, peeled, pitted and diced
- 1 1/2 tablespoons pine nuts

1. Preheat air fryer at 180°C for 3 minutes.
2. In a small bowl, combine carrot, apple cider vinegar, ginger and cayenne. Set aside.
3. In a separate small bowl, combine onion, parsnip and avocado oil. Set aside.
4. In a medium bowl, combine tofu, five-spice powder and chilli powder.
5. Place onion mixture in air fryer basket lightly greased with olive oil. Cook for 6 minutes. Add tofu mixture and toss. Cook for an additional 8 minutes. Stir in lime zest.
6. Prepare Buddha Bowls by evenly distributing rocket, drained carrot juliennes, riced cauliflower, avocado, pine nuts and tofu mixture between two medium bowls. Serve.

PER SERVING

KILOJOULES: 766 | **FAT:** 13g | **PROTEIN:** 6g | **SODIUM:** 48mg | **FIBRE:** 6g | **CARBOHYDRATES:** 14g | **NET CARBOHYDRATES:** 8g | **SUGAR:** 4g

Curried Tofu and Turmeric Cauli Rice

To ensure nice and crispy tofu, both drain it and use paper towels to gently press the excess moisture out before cutting the tofu into cubes.

Hands-On Time: 5 minutes
Cook Time: 16 minutes

Serves 4

- 230 grams extra-firm tofu, pressed and cut into 6mm cubes
- 1/2 cup canned unsweetened coconut milk
- 2 teaspoons red curry paste
- 2 cloves garlic, peeled and minced
- 3/4 tablespoon avocado oil
- 3/4 tablespoon coconut oil
- 1 small head cauliflower, pulsed into rice
- 3/4 tablespoon turmeric powder
- 1/2 teaspoon salt
- 1/2 teaspoon freshly ground white pepper
- 4 lime wedges
- 1/4 cup chopped fresh coriander

1. In a medium bowl, combine tofu, coconut milk, red curry paste, garlic and avocado oil. Refrigerate covered 30 minutes.
2. Preheat air fryer at 180°C for 3 minutes.
3. Place tofu and marinade in an ungreased cake barrel. Place in air fryer basket and cook for 5 minutes. Stir, then cook for an additional 5 minutes.
4. While tofu is cooking, heat coconut oil in a medium frying pan over medium-high heat for 30 seconds. Add riced cauliflower, turmeric powder, salt and pepper. Stir-fry for 6 minutes until cauliflower is tender to your preference.
5. Add cauliflower to four medium bowls. Top with tofu mixture and sauce. Garnish with lime wedges and cilantro. Serve warm.

PER SERVING

KILOJOULES: 740 | **FAT:** 12g | **PROTEIN:** 9g | **SODIUM:** 532mg | **FIBRE:** 4g | **CARBOHYDRATES:** 12g | **NET CARBOHYDRATES:** 7g | **SUGAR:** 3g

Korean Ground "Beef" and Kimchi Bowls

Packed with beautiful flavours, this dish would be great over a bed of low-carb cauliflower rice or zoodles. Add a little coconut aminos to either of these bases when heating up.

Hands-On Time: 10 minutes
Cook Time: 8 minutes

Serves 4

- **2 cups plant-based mince**
- **1 medium carrot, peeled and julienned**
- **6 spring onions, sliced, 2 tablespoons greens reserved for garnish**
- **1 medium zucchini, diced**
- **1 1/2 tablespoons coconut aminos**
- **2 teaspoons sesame oil**
- **1 teaspoon apple cider vinegar**
- **2 teaspoons erythritol sweetener**
- **3/4 tablespoon gochujang**
- **1/4 teaspoon salt**
- **1/2 cup kimchi**
- **2 teaspoons roasted sesame seeds**

WHERE DO I FIND ROASTED SESAME SEEDS?

You can purchase pre-roasted sesame seeds in most supermarkets. However, if you can find only unroasted ones, it's easy to roast them yourself. Place your unroasted seeds in a small ungreased frying pan over low heat. Using a spatula, push the seeds around in the skillet until they are golden brown, for about 3 minutes.

1. Preheat air fryer at 180°C for 3 minutes.
2. In a large bowl, combine plant-based mince, carrot, spring onions, zucchini, coconut aminos, sesame oil, apple cider vinegar, erythritol, gochujang and salt.
3. Place mixture in an ungreased cake barrel. Place barrel in air fryer basket and cook for 6 minutes. Stir in kimchi. Cook for an additional 2 minutes.
4. Transfer to two medium bowls and garnish with reserved spring onions and roasted sesame seeds. Serve.

PER SERVING

KILOJOULES: 656 | **FAT:** 7g | **PROTEIN:** 15g | **SODIUM:** 762mg | **FIBRE:** 4g | **CARBOHYDRATES:** 14g | **NET CARBOHYDRATES:** 8g | **SUGAR:** 6g

Caprese Hasselback Tomatoes

With this recipe, you don't want the cheese to be completely melted. The air fryer simply softens up the mozzarella while heating the tomatoes just enough to bring out their natural sugars. And don't forget to use fresh basil leaves — they are everything in a caprese dish!

Hands-On Time: 10 minutes
Cook Time: 3 minutes

Serves 4

- 4 medium Roma tomatoes, bottoms removed to create flat surfaces
- 16 fresh basil leaves
- 230 gram ball fresh mozzarella, sliced and then cut into 16 pieces
- 1/2 teaspoon salt
- 1/2 teaspoon freshly ground black pepper
- 3/4 tablespoon olive oil
- 2 teaspoons balsamic vinegar

1. Preheat air fryer at 160°C for 3 minutes.
2. Make four even slices on each tomato, three-quarters of the way down. Stuff one basil leaf and a piece of mozzarella into each slice. Season with salt and pepper.
3. Place stuffed tomatoes in ungreased air fryer basket. Cook for 3 minutes. Transfer to a large serving plate.
4. Drizzle tomatoes with olive oil and balsamic vinegar and serve.

PER SERVING

KILOJOULES: 841 | **FAT:** 15g | **PROTEIN:** 12g | **SODIUM:** 522mg | **FIBRE:** 2g | **CARBOHYDRATES:** 5g | **NET CARBOHYDRATES:** 4g | **SUGAR:** 4g

Stuffed Capsicum

Capsicums are one of those vegetables that take on a different flavour once cooked. Tender and flavourful, these capsicums are stuffed with a blend of tomatoes, onions, squash and seasonings, with the addition of mushrooms to lend a "meaty" touch.

Hands-On Time: 15 minutes
Cook Time: 22 minutes

Serves 4

- **2 medium capsicums, colour of choice**
- **4 teaspoons olive oil, divided**
- **½ medium brown onion, peeled and finely diced**
- **¾ cup finely diced summer squash**
- **¾ cup chopped Swiss brown mushrooms**
- **½ cup canned fire-roasted diced tomatoes, including juice**
- **¼ cup tomato sauce**
- **2 teaspoons Italian seasoning**
- **¼ teaspoon smoked paprika**
- **½ teaspoon salt**
- **¼ teaspoon freshly ground black pepper**

1. Cut capsicums in half from top to bottom and seed them. Brush inside and tops of capsicums with 2 teaspoons olive oil. Set aside.
2. In a frying pan, heat remaining oil over medium-high heat for 30 seconds. Add onion, squash and mushrooms. Stir-fry for 5 minutes until onions are tender.
3. In a medium bowl, combine tomatoes, tomato sauce, Italian seasoning, smoked paprika, salt and pepper.
4. Preheat air fryer at 180°C for 3 minutes.
5. Evenly distribute mixture among the capsicum halves.
6. Place two halves in the air fryer basket. Cook for 8 minutes.
7. Transfer to a serving plate. Continue with remaining halves. Serve warm.

PER SERVING

KILOJOULES: 339 | **FAT:** 5g | **PROTEIN:** 2g | **SODIUM:** 409mg | **FIBRE:** 3g | **CARBOHYDRATES:** 8g | **NET CARBOHYDRATES:** 6g | **SUGAR:** 5g

Creamy Pesto Spaghetti Squash

Once cooked, the long strands of squash that resemble spaghetti noodles will be easily pulled out — and even spun around on your fork in true Italian fashion!

Hands-On Time: 5 minutes
Cook Time: 25 minutes

Serves 4

2 teaspoons olive oil
680 gram spaghetti squash, halved and seeded
½ teaspoon salt, divided
½ cup pesto
½ cup ricotta cheese
1 ½ tablespoons chopped fresh basil leaves

1. Preheat air fryer at 190°C for 3 minutes.
2. Rub olive oil over both halves of spaghetti squash. Season with half of salt. Place both halves, flat sides down, in ungreased air fryer basket. Cook for 25 minutes.
3. Transfer squash to a cutting board and let cool for 5 minutes until easy to handle. Once cooled, use a fork to gently pull the strands out of squash and place into a medium bowl.
4. Toss squash noodles with pesto, ricotta cheese and remaining salt. Garnish with basil leaves. Serve warm.

PER SERVING

KILOJOULES: 1017 | **FAT:** 20g | **PROTEIN:** 6g | **SODIUM:** 647mg | **FIBRE:** 3g | **CARBOHYDRATES:** 12g | **NET CARBOHYDRATES:** 10g | **SUGAR:** 5g

HOMEMADE PESTO

Although there are several great varieties of pesto on the market, you can also make your own. For a traditional pesto, pulse the following ingredients together: 1 cup fresh basil leaves, ¼ cup fresh parsley, ⅛ teaspoon salt, 4 cloves peeled garlic, ¼ cup raw pine nuts, ½ cup Parmesan cheese (substitute ¼ cup nutritional yeast if you don't eat cheese) and 3 tablespoons olive oil.

Baba Ghanoush

This bold and flavourful Middle Eastern eggplant dish is not only tasty but also so healthy — and so surprisingly low-carb! The air fryer helps lend that smoky element to this classic dip.

Hands-On Time: 5 minutes
Cook Time: 27 minutes

Serves 4

- **3 teaspoons olive oil, divided**
- **1 medium eggplant, halved lengthwise**
- **2 teaspoons pine nuts**
- **1/4 cup tahini**
- **3/4 tablespoon lemon juice**
- **2 cloves garlic, peeled and minced**
- **1/8 teaspoon ground cumin**
- **1/4 teaspoon salt**
- **1/8 teaspoon freshly ground black pepper**
- **1 tablespoon chopped fresh parsley**

1. Preheat air fryer at 190°C for 3 minutes.
2. Rub 2 teaspoons olive oil over both eggplant halves. Pierce eggplant flesh a few times with a fork. Place eggplant, flat sides down, in ungreased air fryer basket. Cook for 25 minutes.
3. Transfer eggplant to a cutting board and let cool for 3 minutes until easy to handle.
4. While eggplant cools, add pine nuts to ungreased air fryer basket. Cook for 2 minutes, shaking every 30 seconds to ensure they don't burn. Set aside in a small bowl.
5. Scoop out eggplant flesh and add to a food processor. Pulse together with tahini, lemon juice, garlic, cumin, salt and pepper. Transfer to a medium serving bowl. Garnish with roasted pine nuts, parsley and remaining olive oil. Serve.

PER SERVING

KILOJOULES: 695 | **FAT:** 13g | **PROTEIN:** 4g | **SODIUM:** 154mg | **FIBRE:** 5g | **CARBOHYDRATES:** 12g | **NET CARBOHYDRATES:** 8g | **SUGAR:** 4g

WHAT ARE CRUDITÉS?

Crudités is just a fancy word for chopped vegetables. So, cut up some carrots, celery, cauliflower, cucumbers, radishes and capsicums — or whatever other vegetables your taste buds desire — and you have yourself a freshly-chopped crudités treat, which is a great companion to this recipe. You are limited only by the produce section!

Spaghetti Squash with Avocado Sauce

The avocado sauce is so creamy and the nutritional yeast gives a hint of cheese flavour. Cooked mushrooms would also be a great addition to this recipe.

Hands-On Time: 5 minutes
Cook Time: 25 minutes

Serves 4

- **2 teaspoons olive oil**
- **680 gram spaghetti squash, halved and seeded**
- **1 teaspoon salt, divided**
- **1 medium ripe avocado, peeled and pitted**
- **$\frac{1}{3}$ cup vegetable broth**
- **2 teaspoons nutritional yeast**
- **2 medium Campari tomatoes, diced**

1. Preheat air fryer at 190°C for 3 minutes.
2. Rub olive oil over both halves of spaghetti squash. Season with $\frac{3}{4}$ teaspoon salt. Place flat sides down in ungreased air fryer basket. Cook for 25 minutes.
3. While squash is cooking, blend together avocado, vegetable broth, nutritional yeast and remaining $\frac{1}{4}$ teaspoon salt. Set aside.
4. Transfer cooked squash to a cutting board and let cool for 4 minutes until easy to handle. Once cooled, use a fork to gently pull strands out of squash into a medium serving bowl. Toss with avocado sauce. Garnish with fresh tomato.

PER SERVING

KILOJOULES: 635 | **FAT:** 10g | **PROTEIN:** 3g | **SODIUM:** 672mg | **FIBRE:** 6g | **CARBOHYDRATES:** 17g | **NET CARBOHYDRATES:** 10g | **SUGAR:** 5g

Chilli-Roasted Vegetable Bowls

These hearty bowls of vegetables are enhanced with a little kick of chilli flavour. Don't be afraid to experiment with your favourite vegetables!

Hands-On Time: 15 minutes
Cook Time: 15 minutes

Serves 4

- **1 cup quartered Brussels sprouts**
- **1 cup broccoli florets**
- **½ small brown onion, peeled and sliced into half-moons**
- **1 medium red capsicum, seeded and sliced**
- **1 medium yellow capsicum, seeded and sliced**
- **¾ tablespoon olive oil**
- **½ teaspoon chilli powder**
- **¼ teaspoon ground cumin**
- **¼ teaspoon ground coriander**

1. Preheat air fryer at 180°C for 3 minutes.
2. In a large bowl, combine Brussels sprouts, broccoli, onion and capsiums. Toss with olive oil, chili powder, cumin and coriander.
3. Add vegetable mixture to ungreased air fryer basket. Cook for 15 minutes, tossing every 5 minutes.
4. Transfer to four medium bowls and serve warm.

PER SERVING

KILOJOULES: 293 | **FAT:** 4g | **PROTEIN:** 2g | **SODIUM:** 23mg | **FIBRE:** 3g | **CARBOHYDRATES:** 8g | **NET CARBOHYDRATES:** 5g | **SUGAR:** 4g

"Fauxtato" Shepherdless Pie

This pie delivers all the punch of the classic version, without the meat and carbs. The rich filling is topped with a creamy and cheesy mashed "fauxtato" topping. For a decorative effect, pipe dollops of the mashed "fauxtatoes" on top before cooking.

Hands-On Time: 15 minutes
Cook Time: 23 minutes

Serves 6

For Topping

- 1/2 small head cauliflower, cut into florets
- 1 small parsnip, peeled and diced
- 3/4 tablespoon avocado oil
- 1/4 cup nondairy shredded Cheddar
- 1 1/2 tablespoons almond milk
- 1/2 teaspoon salt
- 1/2 teaspoon freshly ground black pepper

For Filling

- 2 teaspoons avocado oil
- 1 cup plant based mince
- 1/2 small brown onion, peeled and diced
- 2 cloves garlic, peeled and minced
- 1 medium carrot, peeled and diced
- 1/4 cup seeded and diced green capsicum
- 1 small stalk celery, diced
- 2/3 cup no-sugar-added tomato sauce
- 1 teaspoon chopped fresh rosemary
- 1 teaspoon fresh thyme leaves
- 1/2 teaspoon salt
- 1/2 teaspoon freshly ground black pepper

1. **To make Topping:** Add cauliflower and parsnip to a medium pot of salted boiling water over high heat for 7 minutes until fork-tender.
2. Drain cauliflower and parsnip and transfer to a medium bowl. Add avocado oil, Cheddar, almond milk, salt and pepper. Mash until smooth.
3. **To make Filling:** While cauliflower and parsnips are cooking, add avocado oil to a large frying pan over medium-high heat. Toss in plant based mince, onion, garlic, carrot, capsicum and celery and cook for 4 minutes until vegetables are tender. Add tomato sauce, rosemary, thyme, salt and black pepper. Set aside.
4. **To assemble:** Preheat air fryer at 180°C for 3 minutes.
5. Spoon filling into a round cake barrel lightly greased with olive oil. Top with topping. Using the tines of a fork, run shallow lines in the top of the cauliflower for a decorative touch. Cook for 12 minutes.
6. Remove barrel from air fryer and let rest for 10 minutes in barrel, then serve warm.

PER SERVING

KILOJOULES: 569 | **FAT:** 7g | **PROTEIN:** 6g | **SODIUM:** 655mg | **FIBRE:** 3g | **CARBOHYDRATES:** 12g | **NET CARBOHYDRATES:** 9g | **SUGAR:** 4g

Broccoli Casserole

People who don't really care for broccoli will find themselves scooping up a second helping of this creamy casserole.

Hands-On Time: 15 minutes
Cook Time: 14 minutes

Serves 4

- 4 cups steamed broccoli florets (about 1 large head), chopped
- 1/4 cup peeled diced brown onion
- 1/2 cup diced white mushrooms
- 1 large egg
- 1 1/2 tablespoons sour cream
- 1/4 cup mayonnaise
- 1 teaspoon salt
- 1/2 teaspoon freshly ground black pepper
- 1 cup coarsely crushed Cheddar cheese crisps

1. In a large bowl, combine broccoli, onion, mushrooms, egg, sour cream, mayonnaise, salt and pepper. Spoon mixture into a round cake barrel.
2. Preheat air fryer at 180°C for 3 minutes.
3. Cook casserole for 14 minutes.
4. Remove barrel from air fryer and let rest for 10 minutes. Evenly distribute crushed Cheddar cheese crisps over the top of casserole and serve warm.

PER SERVING

KILOJOULES: 1050 | **FAT:** 21g | **PROTEIN:** 10g | **SODIUM:** 896mg | **FIBRE:** 3g | **CARBOHYDRATES:** 8g | **NET CARBOHYDRATES:** 6g | **SUGAR:** 2g

Vegan Dogs and Sauerkraut

Your air fryer is the perfect appliance for cooking hot dogs. When you want that grill flavour, but don't have the time, just break out the air fryer and in no time you will be on your very own personal picnic.

Hands-On Time: 5 minutes
Cook Time: 5 minutes

Serves 2

4 vegan hot dogs
2 cups sauerkraut
1 ½ tablespoons German mustard

HOMEMADE SAUERKRAUT
Fermenting vegetables can seem very scary to those who have never tried it. Let sauerkraut be your gateway into a fun new world. Sauerkraut consists of just two ingredients: cabbage and salt. You'll find all the details online for fermenting your own in a few easy steps.

1. Preheat air fryer to 200°C for 3 minutes.
2. Add hot dogs to ungreased air fryer basket. Cook for 5 minutes.
3. Transfer hot dogs to a large plate and serve warm with sauerkraut and mustard.

PER SERVING

KILOJOULES: 573 | **FAT:** 2g | **PROTEIN:** 16g | **SODIUM:** 1,965mg | **FIBRE:** 6g | **CARBOHYDRATES:** 16g | **NET CARBOHYDRATES:** 10g | **SUGAR:** 6g

9

Desserts

Enjoying sweet treats can seem almost impossible when eating a low-carb diet. All of those cakes, pies, cobblers and cookies are usually filled with one pesky, carb-filled ingredient: sugar. But that doesn't mean you have to ignore your sweet tooth. In fact, there are dozens of sugar substitutes available that allow you to create low-carb desserts that are just as yummy as the original recipes — if not more so. And the air fryer is here to make them even easier to bake!

With recipes ranging from Ultimate Chocolate Brownies and Blueberry Crumble Jars to Nutty Pumpkin Mug Cake, the mouthwatering delights in this chapter are guaranteed to hit the spot — no matter what you find yourself craving.

Ultimate Chocolate Brownies

What is better than chocolate? Double chocolate! And the crunch of the pecans is a natural addition to these brownies, although crushed almonds or walnuts work just as well! For presentation, dust a little powdered erythritol on the finished bake.

Hands-On Time: 10 minutes
Cook Time: 11 minutes

Makes 9 brownies

- **1/3 cup almond flour**
- **1/4 cup unsweetened cocoa**
- **1/2 cup powdered erythritol**
- **1/2 teaspoon baking soda**
- **2 1/4 tablespoons unsalted butter, melted**
- **3/4 tablespoon sour cream**
- **1 large egg**
- **1/8 teaspoon salt**
- **1/4 cup no sugar chocolate chips**
- **1/4 cup chopped pecans**

1. Preheat air fryer at 180°C for 3 minutes.
2. In a medium bowl, combine flour, cocoa, erythritol, baking soda, butter and sour cream. Stir in egg and salt. Add chocolate chips and chopped pecans, stirring until mixture is thick and sticky.
3. Press mixture into a square cake barrel greased with cooking spray. Cover pan with aluminium foil and place in air fryer basket. Cook for 9 minutes. Remove foil and cook for an additional 2 minutes.
4. Remove pan from air fryer and let cool for 30 minutes. Once cooled, slice into nine sections and serve.

PER SERVING (1 BROWNIE)

KILOJOULES: 527 | **FAT:** 11g | **PROTEIN:** 3g | **SODIUM:** 63mg | **FIBRE:** 2g | **CARBOHYDRATES:** 18g | **NET CARBOHYDRATES:** 2g | **SUGAR:** 0g

Giant Chocolate Chip Cookie

This chocolate chip cookie is thinner than a cake but thicker than a cookie — with all the flavour you love. Top with sugar-free whipped cream for an extra special treat.

Hands-On Time: 10 minutes
Cook Time: 8 minutes

Makes 9 cookies

- 1/3 cup almond flour
- 1 1/2 tablespoons erythritol sweetener
- 1 large egg
- 1/2 teaspoon vanilla extract
- 2 1/4 tablespoons butter, melted
- 1/8 teaspoon salt
- 2 tablespoons sugar-free dark chocolate chips

1. Preheat air fryer at 180°C for 3 minutes.
2. In a medium bowl, combine all ingredients except chocolate chips. Fold in chocolate chips.
3. Spoon mixture into a pizza pan greased with cooking spray. Place pan in air fryer basket and cook for 8 minutes.
4. Slice and serve warm.

PER SERVING (1 COOKIE)

KILOJOULES: 343 | **FAT:** 7g | **PROTEIN:** 2g | **SODIUM:** 42mg | **FIBRE:** 1g | **CARBOHYDRATES:** 6g | **NET CARBOHYDRATES:** 1g | **SUGAR:** 0g

Giant Peanut Butter Cookie

The powdered peanut butter contains less natural fat because the peanuts have been pressed down and then ground into a fine powder. It lends a peanut butter flavour to cookies, smoothies and even low-carb pancakes!

Hands-On Time: 10 minutes
Cook Time: 8 minutes

Makes 9 cookies

- 1/3 cup almond flour
- 1/4 cup powdered erythritol
- 1 large egg
- 1/2 teaspoon vanilla extract
- 3 tablespoons butter, melted
- 1/8 teaspoon salt
- 3 tablespoons powdered peanut butter

1. Preheat air fryer at 180°C for 3 minutes.
2. In a medium bowl, combine all ingredients.
3. Spoon mixture into a pizza pan greased with cooking spray. Place pan in air fryer basket and cook for 8 minutes.
4. Slice and serve warm.

PER SERVING (1 COOKIE)

KILOJOULES: 372 | **FAT:** 8g | **PROTEIN:** 3g | **SODIUM:** 63mg | **FIBRE:** 1g | **CARBOHYDRATES:** 7g | **NET CARBOHYDRATES:** 1g | **SUGAR:** 0g

Strawberry Cake with Orange Glaze

This fresh cake is filled with chopped strawberries, lending a moistness to every bite. The orange in the glaze pairs nicely with the berry flavour. Pour a cup of tea, pull up a chair and cut yourself a slice!

Hands-On Time: 10 minutes
Cook Time: 10 minutes

Serves 4

For Cake
- 1/2 cup finely ground almond flour
- 1/4 cup powdered erythritol sweetener
- 1/2 teaspoon baking powder
- 1/8 teaspoon salt
- 1 1/2 tablespoons butter, melted
- 1 large egg
- 2 teaspoons orange zest
- 1/2 teaspoon unflavoured gelatin
- 1/2 teaspoon vanilla extract
- 1/2 teaspoon ground cinnamon
- 1/4 cup hulled and finely chopped strawberries

For Glaze
- 3/4 tablespoon butter, melted
- 1/4 teaspoon orange zest
- 1 tablespoon orange juice
- 1/4 cup powdered erythritol sweetener

1. **To make Cake:** Preheat air fryer at 150°C for 3 minutes.
2. In a large bowl, combine flour, erythritol, baking powder and salt. Set aside.
3. In a small bowl, combine butter, egg, orange zest, gelatin, vanilla, cinnamon and strawberries. Add to flour mixture and stir until combined.
4. Spoon mixture into an ungreased pizza pan. Place pan in air fryer basket and cook for 10 minutes. Remove pan from basket and let set for about 30 minutes until cooled.
5. **To make Glaze:** Combine butter, orange zest, orange juice and erythritol in a small bowl. Add a little water if glaze is too thick and a little extra erythritol if glaze is too thin. Pour over cooled cake.
6. Slice cake and serve.

PER SERVING

KILOJOULES: 765 | **FAT:** 17g | **PROTEIN:** 5g | **SODIUM:** 143mg | **FIBRE:** 2g | **CARBOHYDRATES:** 29 | **NET CARBOHYDRATES:** 3g | **SUGAR:** 2g

Almond Ricotta Lime Cake

This bright and tasty low-carb delicacy is an ideal dessert for any night of the week or even a nice start to your day alongside a warm cup of tea or coffee.

Hands-On Time: 5 minutes
Cook Time: 15 minutes

Serves 2

For Cake

- 1 cup finely ground almond flour
- 1/3 cup powdered erythritol sweetener
- 1 teaspoon baking powder
- 1/2 teaspoon cream of tartar
- 1/8 teaspoon salt
- 2 large eggs
- 1/2 cup ricotta cheese
- 3/4 tablespoon butter, melted
- 1/2 teaspoon vanilla extract
- 1/2 teaspoon lime zest
- 1 tablespoon lime juice

For Topping

- 1 tablespoon butter, melted
- 1/4 teaspoon lime zest
- 2 teaspoons lime juice
- 1/4 cup plus 1 tablespoon powdered erythritol sweetener, divided
- 1 1/2 tablespoons sliced almonds

1. **To make Cake:** Preheat air fryer at 150°C for 3 minutes.
2. In a large bowl, combine flour, erythritol, baking powder, cream of tartar and salt. Stir in eggs, ricotta cheese, butter, vanilla, lime zest and lime juice until combined.
3. Spoon mixture into a 18cm springform pan greased with cooking spray. Place pan in air fryer basket and cook for 15 minutes.
4. Remove pan from basket and let cool for 10 minutes, then remove sides of springform pan.
5. **To make Topping:** Combine butter, lime zest, lime juice and 1/4 cup erythritol in a small bowl. Consistency should be a little thicker than a glaze. Spread over top of cooled cake.
6. Garnish with almonds and remaining erythritol. Slice and serve.

PER SERVING

KILOJOULES: 2694 | **FAT:** 55g | **PROTEIN:** 27g | **SODIUM:** 472mg | **FIBRE:** 7g | **CARBOHYDRATES:** 80g | **NET CARBOHYDRATES:** 11g | **SUGAR:** 3g

Double Chocolate Cake

When chocolate is screaming your name but you don't want the sugar, this low-carb cake for two will hit your craving in the right place. It's also great with a scoop of sugar-free ice cream!

Hands-On Time: 5 minutes
Cook Time: 15 minutes

Serves 2

For Cake

- 2/3 cup finely ground almond flour
- 1/4 cup cocoa
- 1/3 cup powdered erythritol sweetener
- 1 teaspoon baking powder
- 1/8 teaspoon salt
- 1/8 teaspoon ground cinnamon
- 1/8 teaspoon chilli powder
- 3 tablespoons butter, melted
- 2 large eggs
- 1 teaspoon vanilla extract

For Chocolate Ganache

- 1/4 cup no sugar chocolate chips
- 1 1/2 tablespoons thickened cream
- 3/4 tablespoon powdered erythritol

1. **To make Cake:** Preheat air fryer at 180°C for 3 minutes.
2. In a large bowl, combine flour, cocoa, erythritol, baking powder, salt, cinnamon and chilli powder. Set aside.
3. In a small bowl, combine butter, eggs and vanilla. Add to flour mixture and stir until smooth.
4. Spoon mixture into a cake barrel lightly greased with olive oil. Place barrel in air fryer basket and cook for 11 minutes.
5. Remove barrel from basket and let set until cool, about 10 minutes.
6. **To make Chocolate Ganache:** In a double boiler, add all ingredients and place over medium heat. Continuously whisk mixture until smooth, about 4 minutes.
7. Pour ganache over cooled cake and let set for 30 minutes. Slice and serve.

PER SERVING

KILOJOULES: 2979 | **FAT:** 62g | **PROTEIN:** 19g | **SODIUM:** 426mg | **FIBRE:** 10g | **CARBOHYDRATES:** 72g | **NET CARBOHYDRATES:** 10g | **SUGAR:** 2g

Blueberry Crumble Jars

Serve this portable low-carb delight with some fresh whipped cream or sugar-free vanilla ice cream.

Hands-On Time: 10 minutes
Cook Time: 24 minutes

Serves 6

For Blueberry Filling

- 3 cups fresh blueberries
- 1 1/2 tablespoons almond flour
- 3/4 tablespoon pulp-free orange juice
- 2 teaspoons orange zest
- 1/4 cup erythritol sweetener
- 3/4 tablespoon butter, melted
- 1/8 teaspoon salt
- 6 (110 gram) oven-safe glass jelly jars

For Crumble Topping

- 1 1/2 tablespoons almond flour
- 1 1/2 tablespoons erythritol sweetener
- 3 tablespoons pecan pieces
- 1 1/2 tablespoons slivered almonds
- 1 1/2 tablespoons unsweetened coconut flakes
- 1 1/2 tablespoons unsalted sunflower seeds
- 2 1/4 tablespoons butter, melted

1. **To make Blueberry Filling:** Preheat air fryer at 180°C for 3 minutes.
2. Combine all ingredients in a large bowl. Distribute evenly into jam jars.
3. Place three jars in air fryer basket. Cook for 7 minutes. Repeat cooking with remaining jars. When jars are removed from air fryer, use the back of a spoon to gently press down on the blueberry filling. Set aside.
4. **To make Crumble Topping:** Combine all ingredients in a medium bowl. Distribute mixture over cooked filling in jars.
5. Place three jars back in air fryer and cook for an additional 5 minutes. Repeat cooking with remaining jars.
6. Let jars cool for 10 minutes before eating or covering. Refrigerate until ready to serve, up to four days.

PER SERVING

KILOJOULES: 853 | **FAT:** 16g | **PROTEIN:** 3g | **SODIUM:** 57mg | **FIBRE:** 3g | **CARBOHYDRATES:** 27g | **NET CARBOHYDRATES:** 11g | **SUGAR:** 9g

USING JAM JARS

Jam jars are traditionally used for canning but serve other purposes as well. By making desserts in these jars, it not only pre-portions your recipes, but it also makes them portable for easy grab-and-go lunch additions.

Ginger Strawberry Crumble Jars

The freshly grated ginger in this dessert adds a zippy counterpart to the fresh, sweet strawberries. Already portioned out, the jars are easy to store and bring along for a picnic, hike or your lunchbox!

Hands-On Time: 10 minutes
Cook Time: 24 minutes

Serves 6

For Filling

- 3 cups hulled and small-diced fresh strawberries
- 1 1/2 tablespoons almond flour
- 2 teaspoons peeled and grated fresh ginger
- 1 tablespoon lime juice
- 2 teaspoons lime zest
- 1/4 cup erythritol sweetener
- 1 tablespoon butter, melted
- 1/8 teaspoon salt
- 6 (110 gram) glass jam jars

For Crumble Topping

- 1 1/2 tablespoons almond flour
- 1 1/2 tablespoons erythritol sweetener
- 1 teaspoon peeled and grated fresh ginger
- 3 tablespoons pecan pieces
- 1 1/2 tablespoons slivered almonds
- 1 1/2 tablespoons unsweetened coconut flakes
- 1 1/2 tablespoons unsalted sunflower seeds
- 2 1/4 tablespoons butter, melted

1. **To make Filling:** Preheat air fryer at 180°C for 3 minutes.
2. Combine strawberries, almond flour, ginger, lime juice, lime zest, erythritol, butter and salt in a medium bowl. Distribute into jam jars.
3. Place three jars in air fryer basket. Cook for 7 minutes. Repeat cooking with remaining jars. When jars are removed from air fryer, use the back of a spoon and gently press down on the strawberry filling. Set aside.
4. **To make Crumble Topping:** Combine all ingredients in a medium bowl. Distribute mixture on top of cooked filling.
5. Add three jars back to air fryer and cook for an additional 5 minutes. Repeat cooking with remaining jars.
6. Let jars cool for 10 minutes before eating or covering. Refrigerate until ready to serve, up to four days.

PER SERVING

KILOJOULES: 803 | **FAT:** 17g | **PROTEIN:** 3g | **SODIUM:** 53mg | **FIBRE:** 4g | **CARBOHYDRATES:** 22g | **NET CARBOHYDRATES:** 6g | **SUGAR:** 5g

Key Lime Cheesecake

Key limes tend to be seasonal — if you can't find any in the supermarket just substitute for half lime juice and half lemon juice. In fact, most any citrus fruit will yield a tasty treat — try blood oranges for an exotic twist.

Hands-On Time: 10 minutes
Cook Time: 19 minutes

Serves 6

- **1 cup ground walnuts (walnut meal)**
- **2 1/4 tablespoons butter, melted**
- **2 1/4 tablespoons erythritol sweetener**
- **340 grams cream cheese, room temperature**
- **1 1/2 tablespoons sour cream**
- **2 large eggs**
- **1/4 cup powdered erythritol sweetener**
- **3/4 tablespoon key lime zest**
- **3/4 tablespoon fresh key lime juice**
- **1 teaspoon vanilla extract**
- **1/8 teaspoon salt**

1. Preheat air fryer at 200°C for 3 minutes.
2. Combine ground walnuts, butter and granular erythritol in a medium bowl. Press mixture into an ungreased 18cm springform pan.
3. Place pan in air fryer basket and bake for 5 minutes. Set aside.
4. In a separate medium bowl, combine cream cheese, sour cream, eggs, powdered erythritol, lime zest, lime juice, vanilla and salt until smooth. Spoon mixture over cooked crust. Cover with aluminium foil.
5. Place springform pan in air fryer basket and cook for 14 minutes.
6. Remove aluminium foil and cook for an additional 5 minutes at 180°C. Cheesecake will be a little jiggly in the centre when done.
7. Refrigerate for at least 2 hours to allow to set. Once set, release sides of pan and serve.

PER SERVING

KILOJOULES: 1552 | **FAT:** 36g | **PROTEIN:** 8g | **SODIUM:** 253mg | **FIBRE:** 1g | **CARBOHYDRATES:** 20g | **NET CARBOHYDRATES:** 5g | **SUGAR:** 3g

Vanilla Cheesecake with Blackberry Sauce

If you really want a fresh vanilla punch with this cheesecake, use a fresh vanilla bean. As a simple substitution, you can use 2 teaspoons vanilla extract instead.

Hands-On Time: 10 minutes
Cook Time: 29 minutes

Serves 6

For Cheesecake

- 1 cup ground walnuts (walnut meal)
- 2 1/4 tablespoons butter, melted
- 2 1/4 tablespoons erythritol sweetener
- 340 grams cream cheese, room temperature
- 1 1/2 tablespoons sour cream
- 2 large eggs
- 1/4 cup powdered erythritol sweetener
- Seeds from 1 vanilla bean
- 1/8 teaspoon salt

For Blackberry Sauce

- 1 1/2 cups fresh blackberries
- 1 1/2 tablespoons lemon juice
- 1/2 cup erythritol sweetener

1. **To make Cheesecake:** Preheat air fryer at 200°C for 3 minutes.
2. Combine ground walnuts, butter and granular erythritol in a medium bowl. Press mixture into an ungreased 18cm springform pan.
3. Place pan in air fryer basket and bake for 5 minutes. Remove from basket and allow to cool for at least 30 minutes.
4. Combine cream cheese, sour cream, eggs, powdered erythritol, vanilla bean seeds and salt in a separate medium bowl. Spoon mixture over cooled crust. Cover with aluminium foil.
5. Place pan back in air fryer basket and cook for 14 minutes. Remove aluminium foil and cook for an additional 5 minutes at 180°C. Refrigerate for at least 2 hours to allow cheesecake to set.
6. **To make Blackberry Sauce:** Place ingredients in a small saucepan and cook over medium heat for 5 minutes. Using the back of a spoon, smoosh berries against saucepan while cooking.
7. After berries are popped and sauce has thickened, press through a sieve to filter out seeds. Refrigerate covered until ready to use.
8. Once cheesecake is cooled and set, release sides of pan and serve chilled with blackberry sauce on top.

PER SERVING

KILOJOULES: 1610 | **FAT:** 37g | **PROTEIN:** 8g | **SODIUM:** 253mg | **FIBRE:** 3g | **CARBOHYDRATES:** 39g | **NET CARBOHYDRATES:** 6g | **SUGAR:** 4g

Dark Chocolate Satin Custard

Smooth and creamy, this custard will send your taste buds to the heavens whenever that carb craving sneaks your way.

Hands-On Time: 15 minutes
Cook Time: 24 minutes

Serves 4

- **4 large egg yolks**
- **1 1/2 tablespoons powdered erythritol sweetener**
- **1/8 teaspoon salt**
- **1/8 teaspoon vanilla extract**
- **1 1/2 cups thickened cream**
- **3/4 cup no sugar dark chocolate chips**
- **1 teaspoon ground cinnamon**

1. In a small bowl, whisk together egg yolks, erythritol, salt and vanilla. Set aside.
2. In a medium saucepan, heat cream over medium-low heat for 4 minutes to a low simmer.
3. Whisk a spoonful of thickened cream into egg mixture to temper eggs, then slowly whisk egg mixture into saucepan with remaining heavy cream. Add chocolate chips and cinnamon and continually stir for 10 minutes on simmer until chocolate is melted.
4. Remove pan from heat and evenly distribute chocolate mixture among four ungreased custard ramekins.
5. Preheat air fryer at 180°C for 3 minutes.
6. Place two ramekins in air fryer basket. Cook for 7 minutes. Transfer ramekins to a cooling rack. Repeat cooking with remaining two ramekins.
7. Allow ramekins to cool for 15 minutes, then refrigerate covered for at least 2 hours before serving.

PER SERVING

KILOJOULES: 2397 | **FAT:** 50g | **PROTEIN:** 8g | **SODIUM:** 105mg | **FIBRE:** 3g | **CARBOHYDRATES:** 37g | **NET CARBOHYDRATES:** 6g | **SUGAR:** 3g

Loco Coco Rum Custard

Taste a bite of vacation with this deliciously rich custard. The rum extract gives a little nod to the tropical coconut drink you'd have while sitting poolside.

Hands-On Time: 15 minutes
Cook Time: 19 minutes

Serves 4

4 large egg yolks
1/4 cup powdered erythritol
1 teaspoon rum extract
1/8 teaspoon salt
380 grams sugar-free coconut cream
1/4 cup thickened cream

1. In a small bowl, whisk together egg yolks, erythritol, rum extract and salt. Set aside.
2. In a medium saucepan, heat coconut cream and thickened cream over medium-low heat for 5 minutes to a low simmer.
3. Whisk a spoonful heated cream mixture into egg mixture to temper eggs, then slowly whisk egg mixture into saucepan with remaining thickened cream.
4. Remove pan from heat and evenly distribute mixture among four ungreased custard ramekins.
5. Preheat air fryer at 180°C for 3 minutes.
6. Place two ramekins in air fryer basket. Cook for 7 minutes. Transfer to a cooling rack and repeat cooking with remaining two ramekins.
7. Allow ramekins to cool for 15 minutes, then refrigerate covered for at least 2 hours before serving.

PER SERVING

KILOJOULES: 1242 | **FAT:** 26g | **PROTEIN:** 5g | **SODIUM:** 100mg | **FIBRE:** 0g | **CARBOHYDRATES:** 16g | **NET CARBOHYDRATES:** 4g | |**SUGAR:** 1g

Lemon Curd Palmiers

From the end result, these look impossible to make for a home chef, but they are actually quite simple, with layers of filo rolled up with "tart-tastic" lemon curd. Try orange curd for a change of pace.

Hands-On Time: 15 minutes
Cook Time: 24 minutes

Serves 9

- **3 3/4 teaspoons erythritol sweetener, divided**
- **1 sheet filo pastry, thawed to room temperature**
- **3/4 tablespoon butter, melted**
- **1/3 cup lemon curd**

HOMEMADE LEMON CURD

Although lemon curd can be purchased jarred in most grocery stores, it can be easily made and is amazingly delicious. Combine 4 large egg yolks and 2/3 cup erythritol sweetener in a small pot over low heat. Whisk in 2/3 cup fresh lemon juice and 1 teaspoon fresh lemon zest. Slowly whisk in 3 3/4 tablespoons unsalted butter, 3/4 tablespoon at a time. Stir continuously until combined and thickened. Strain through a sieve and store covered until ready to use for up to one week.

1. On a flat, clean surface sprinkle 2 teaspoons erythritol over surface. Place filo sheet over scattered erythritol. Brush butter over sheet. Sprinkle with remaining erythritol. Flip dough.
2. Evenly spread lemon curd over sheet. Carefully roll one end toward the middle of sheet. Stop at the halfway point. Roll opposite side toward the middle. Refrigerate covered for 30 minutes.
3. Slice double log into 18 equal slices.
4. Preheat air fryer at 180°C for 3 minutes.
5. Place six palmiers in lightly greased air fryer basket. Cook for 8 minutes. Repeat with remaining palmiers.
6. Transfer cooked palmiers to a cooling rack. Serve warm or at room temperature.

PER SERVING

KILOJOULES: 322 | **FAT:** 3g | **PROTEIN:** 1g | **SODIUM:** 19mg | **FIBRE:** 0g | **CARBOHYDRATES:** 13g | **NET CARBOHYDRATES:** 12g | **SUGAR:** 11g

Nutty Pumpkin Mug Cake

Enjoy this spiced dessert beside the fireplace on a cool autumn night — or wherever and whenever the craving hits! This would be delicious topped with some fresh whipped cream or a scoop of sugar-free ice cream.

Hands-On Time: 5 minutes
Cook Time: 25 minutes

Serves 1

- 1 large egg
- 3/4 tablespoon coconut flour
- 3/4 tablespoon almond flour
- 1 1/2 tablespoons thickened whipping cream
- 1 1/2 tablespoons erythritol sweetener
- 2 teaspoons pumpkin pie spice (see note below)
- 1/4 teaspoon maple extract
- 1/4 teaspoon baking powder
- 1 1/2 tablespoons chopped walnuts
- 1/8 teaspoon salt

1. Preheat air fryer at 150°C for 3 minutes.
2. In a small bowl, whisk egg together with remaining ingredients.
3. Pour batter into a 10cm ramekin greased with cooking spray.
4. Place ramekin in air fryer basket and cook for 25 minutes.
5. Remove ramekin from basket and let set for 5 minutes. Serve warm.

PER SERVING

KILOJOULES: 1481 | **FAT:** 30g | **PROTEIN:** 12g | **SODIUM:** 480mg | **FIBRE:** 5g | **CARBOHYDRATES:** 35g | **NET CARBOHYDRATES:** 7g | **SUGAR:** 3g

WHAT IS PUMPKIN PIE SPICE?

A blend perfect for topping pumpkin pies and other spiced dessert favourites. Simply combining the following ingredients: 3 tablespoons ground cinnamon, 2 teaspoons ground ginger, 1 1/2 teaspoons ground nutmeg, 1 teaspoon ground allspice and 1 teaspoon ground cloves.

Nutty Chocolate Cheesecake

The touch of espresso powder in this recipe enhances the flavour of the chocolate. It's a soon-to-be favourite no one will guess is low-carb!

Hands-On Time: 10 minutes
Cook Time: 24 minutes

Serves 6

- **1 cup ground pecans (pecan meal)**
- **2 1/4 tablespoons butter, melted**
- **2 1/4 tablespoons erythritol sweetener**
- **2 teaspoons instant espresso powder**
- **340 grams cream cheese, room temperature**
- **1 1/2 tablespoons sour cream**
- **2 large eggs**
- **1/4 cup unsweetened cocoa**
- **1/4 cup powdered erythritol sweetener**
- **1 teaspoon vanilla extract**
- **1/8 teaspoon salt**
- **1/4 cup mini no sugar chocolate chips**
- **1/4 cup pecan pieces**

1. Preheat air fryer at 200°C for 3 minutes.
2. Combine ground pecans, butter, granular erythritol and espresso powder in a medium bowl. Press mixture into an ungreased 18cm springform pan.
3. Place pan in air fryer basket and bake for 5 minutes. Remove from basket and allow to cool for 15 minutes.
4. In a separate medium bowl, combine cream cheese, sour cream, eggs, unsweetened cocoa, powdered erythritol, vanilla and salt until smooth. Spoon mixture over crust. Cover with aluminium foil.
5. Place springform pan back into air fryer basket and cook for 14 minutes.
6. Remove aluminium foil and cook for an additional 5 minutes at 180°C.
7. Remove cheesecake from air fryer basket. Garnish with chocolate chips and pecan pieces.
8. Cover cheesecake and refrigerate for at least 2 hours to allow it to set. Once set, release sides of pan and serve.

PER SERVING

KILOJOULES: 1916 | **FAT:** 43g | **PROTEIN:** 10g | **SODIUM:** 253mg | **FIBRE:** 3g | **CARBOHYDRATES:** 28g | **NET CARBOHYDRATES:** 6g | **SUGAR:** 3g

Raspberry Pavlova with Orange Cream

A yummy low-carb twist on the Australian favourite. The crispy exterior and almost marshmallow-like consistency is topped with cream and fresh fruit, and it's sure to please!

Hands-On Time: 15 minutes
Cook Time: 90 minutes

Serves 2

For Pavlova

- 2 large egg whites
- 1/4 teaspoon cream of tartar
- 1/2 cup powdered erythritol
- 1/2 teaspoon pulp-free orange juice
- 1/2 teaspoon vanilla extract

For Topping

- 1/3 cup thickened whipping cream
- 1 teaspoon fresh orange juice
- 1/4 teaspoon orange zest
- 2 tablespoons powdered erythritol sweetener
- 1 cup fresh raspberries

1. Cut a piece of baking paper to the size of a grill pan. Draw a 15cm circle on paper. Flip paper, ink side down, onto grill pan. Set aside.
2. **To make Pavlova:** In a medium metal bowl, beat egg whites with a blender on high. Add cream of tartar, then add erythritol, 1 tablespoon at a time, until stiff peaks form. Add orange juice and vanilla and blend.
3. Preheat air fryer at 110°C for 5 minutes.
4. Spoon or pipe egg whites over parchment paper circle, creating higher edges around perimeter, like a pie crust. There should be a divot in the centre.
5. Add grill pan to air fryer and cook for 60 minutes.
6. Turn off heat, and let pavlova sit in air fryer for an additional 30 minutes.
7. Remove grill pan from air fryer and gently peel off baking paper from bottom of pavlova. Transfer to a large plate.
8. **To make Topping:** In a small bowl, whisk together whipping cream, orange juice, orange zest and erythritol until creamy.
9. Fill pavlova with whipped cream and top with raspberries. Serve.

PER SERVING

KILOJOULES: 799 | **FAT:** 15g | **PROTEIN:** 6g | **SODIUM:** 67m | **FIBRE:** 4g | **CARBOHYDRATES:** 69g | **NET CARBOHYDRATES:** 5g | **SUGAR:** 5g

Chocolate Pavlova with Coffee Crema

Crema is traditionally made with carb-filled buttermilk. Here, the flavour is mimicked with a touch of sour cream.

Hands-On Time: 15 minutes
Cook Time: 90 minutes

Serves 2

For Pavlova

- 2 large egg whites
- 1/4 teaspoon cream of tartar
- 1/2 cup powdered erythritol sweetener
- 3/4 tablespoon unsweetened cocoa powder
- 1 teaspoon instant espresso powder
- 1/2 teaspoon apple cider vinegar
- 1/2 teaspoon vanilla extract

For Topping

- 1/4 cup thickened whipping cream
- 2 tablespoons powdered erythritol sweetener
- 3/4 tablespoon sour cream
- 1 teaspoon instant espresso powder
- 28 grams dark chocolate

1. Cut a piece of baking paper to size of a grill pan. Draw a 15cm circle on paper. Flip paper, ink side down, onto grill pan. Set aside.
2. **To make Pavlova:** In a medium metal bowl, beat egg whites with an immersion blender on high. Add cream of tartar, then add erythritol, 1 tablespoon at a time, and blend until stiff peaks form.
3. Fold in cocoa powder and espresso powder. Blend in apple cider vinegar and vanilla.
4. Preheat air fryer at 110°C for 5 minutes.
5. Spoon or pipe egg whites over baking paper circle, creating higher edges around perimeter, like a pie crust. There should be a divot in the centre.
6. Add grill pan to air fryer and cook for 60 minutes.
7. Turn off heat, and let pavlova stay in air fryer for an additional 30 minutes.
8. Remove grill pan from air fryer and gently peel off baking paper from bottom of pavlova. Transfer to a large plate.
9. **To make Topping:** Whisk together whipping cream and erythritol in a small bowl. Fold in sour cream and espresso powder.
10. Fill pavlova with whipped cream. Using a vegetable peeler, shave chocolate into curls over pavlova and serve.

PER SERVING

KILOJOULES: 1251 | **FAT:** 18g | **PROTEIN:** 6g | **SODIUM:** 69mg | **FIBRE:** 3g | **CARBOHYDRATES:** 70g | **NET CARBOHYDRATES:** 8g | **SUGAR:** 5g

Crustless Orange Cheesecake

The citrus in the orange is so fresh and bright, it helps make this a nice summer dessert.

Hands-On Time: 10 minutes
Cook Time: 19 minutes

Serves 8

340 grams cream cheese, at room temperature
1 1/2 tablespoons sour cream
2 large eggs
1/2 cup erythritol sweetener
3/4 tablespoon fresh orange zest
3/4 tablespoon fresh orange juice
1 teaspoon vanilla extract
1/8 teaspoon salt

1 In a medium bowl, combine cream cheese, sour cream, eggs, erythritol, orange zest, orange juice, vanilla and salt until smooth. Spoon into an ungreased 18cm springform pan. Cover with aluminium foil.

2 Preheat air fryer at 200°C for 3 minutes.

3 Place springform pan into air fryer basket and cook for 14 minutes.

4 Reduce air fryer heat to 180°C, remove aluminium foil and cook for an additional 5 minutes.

5 The cheesecake will be a little jiggly in the centre. Refrigerate covered for a minimum of 2 hours to allow it to set. Release sides from pan and serve.

PER SERVING

KILOJOULES: 732 | **FAT:** 16g | **PROTEIN:** 4g | **SODIUM:** 189mg | **FIBRE:** 0g | **CARBOHYDRATES:** 15g | **NET CARBOHYDRATES:** 3g | **SUGAR:** 2g

Candied Walnuts

These walnuts are a great snack as is, but they also taste delicious as a crunchy addition to yoghurt or salad. Try them on the Chopped Steakhouse Salad (see recipe on page 128).

Hands-On Time: 5 minutes
Cook Time: 16 minutes

Serves 6

1 large egg white, beaten
1/4 teaspoon vanilla extract
1/2 cup Natvia Gold sweetener (brown sugar alternative)
1/4 teaspoon ground cinnamon
1/8 teaspoon salt
3 cups walnut halves

1. Preheat air fryer at 140°C for 3 minutes.
2. In a medium bowl, whisk egg white together with vanilla, brown sugar, cinnamon and salt. Add walnuts and toss until well coated.
3. Place walnuts in air fryer basket lightly greased with olive oil. Cook for 8 minutes. Stir, then cook for an additional 8 minutes.
4. Let cool for 10 minutes, then store in an air-tight container at room temperature until ready to serve.

PER SERVING

KILOJOULES: 1384 | **FAT:** 33g | **PROTEIN:** 8g | **SODIUM:** 59mg | **FIBRE:** 3g | **CARBOHYDRATES:** 7g | **NET CARBOHYDRATES:** 4g | **SUGAR:** 1g

“Grilled” Watermelon

Fruit is a great dessert because of its innate sweetness. And when it is grilled or heated, those natural sugars are enhanced! Enjoy these luscious watermelon cubes after dinner as a light dessert, atop a salad or even blended into a smoothie.

Hands-On Time: 10 minutes
Cook Time: 4 minutes

Serves 4

- **2 teaspoons olive oil**
- **1 ½ tablespoons fresh orange juice**
- **1 teaspoon orange zest**
- **¾ tablespoon erythritol sweetener**
- **⅛ teaspoon salt**
- **4 cups 3cm watermelon cubes**
- **¾ tablespoon chopped fresh mint**

1. Preheat air fryer at 190°C for 3 minutes.
2. In a medium bowl, whisk together olive oil, orange juice, orange zest, erythritol and salt. Toss in watermelon cubes and let marinate for 10 minutes.
3. Add watermelon mixture to ungreased air fryer basket. Cook for 2 minutes. Toss. Cook for an additional 2 minutes.
4. Serve warm or at room temperature, garnished with fresh mint.

PER SERVING

KILOJOULES: 288 | **FAT:** 2g | **PROTEIN:** 1g | **SODIUM:** 74mg | **FIBRE:** 1g | **CARBOHYDRATES:** 15g | **NET CARBOHYDRATES:** 12g | **SUGAR:** 10g

Blueberries Jubilee

This sweet treat is great served over sugar-free ice cream or topped with whipped cream during those late-night cravings. It's also good in the morning with some Greek yoghurt. Or even have it over the Vanilla Cheesecake with Blackberry Sauce (see recipe on page 204) instead of the blackberry sauce!

Hands-On Time: 10 minutes
Cook Time: 9 minutes

Serves 4

- **1 1/2 tablespoons butter, melted**
- **1/4 cup erythritol sweetener**
- **2 teaspoons cream of tartar**
- **3/4 tablespoon fresh orange juice**
- **1/2 teaspoon orange zest**
- **1/8 teaspoon ground cinnamon**
- **1/8 teaspoon salt**
- **2 cups fresh blueberries**

1. Preheat air fryer at 180°C for 3 minutes.
2. In a medium bowl, whisk together butter, erythritol, cream of tartar, orange juice, orange zest, cinnamon and salt. Toss in blueberries. Pour into an ungreased cake barrel.
3. Place cake barrel in air fryer basket. Cook for 9 minutes, stirring every 3 minutes.
4. Enjoy warmed or at room temperature.

PER SERVING

KILOJOULES: 406 | **FAT:** 6g | **PROTEIN:** 1g | **SODIUM:** 75mg | **FIBRE:** 2g | **CARBOHYDRATES:** 24g | **NET CARBOHYDRATES:** 10g | **SUGAR:** 7g

Index

C